# Managing Legal Change Inititatives

EDITED BY EDWARD BOWES

**Commissioning editor**
Laura Armentano

**Editorial assistant**
Edward Bowes

**Published by**
Globe Law and Business Ltd
3 Mylor Close
Horsell
Woking
Surrey GU21 4DD
United Kingdom
Tel: +44 20 3745 4770
www.globelawandbusiness.com

ISBN: 978-1-78358-300-3
A catalogue record for this book is available from the British Library

# Contents

# Executive summary

Successfully managing a change initiative is no simple feat, regardless of the size of the firm – distilling the process of change into a workforce takes careful planning and support. Change is stressful and difficult for people to process and accept, as we often cling to what we know. This is especially true of lawyers, who are notoriously averse to change.

However, the legal sector has begun to rapidly transform – and the firms that don't change with it are going to struggle to stay relevant. In these turbulent times for firms, change initiatives must be properly managed to ensure the whole firm can successfully shift to the new norm and stick to it. Without the proper support and management, a firm runs the risks of alienating their workforce – who will not take well to sudden and imposed change.

*Managing Legal Change Initiatives* looks to illustrate the best methods of introducing and managing change in a sector that is known for being averse to it. The book highlights the critical obstacles and pitfalls that law firms will face during transitional periods, and outlines some of the best methods of approaching organizational change; from building a change framework to follow to encouraging a shift in partner behavior through the compensation strategy. This new book also explores why change is so difficult for individuals – with discussion of the neuroscience behind change, and the role of emotional intelligence in leaders to help garner a transformation.

Chapter 1 features David Parnell , founder and principal of True North Partner Management, exploring why lawyers are so resistant to change, and the best methods of introducing change to them. The hurdles that face a law firm when dealing with a change initiative are explained, and methods that are known to fail are run through. The chapter then moves to discuss how to develop a sense of "urgency" in partner's to bring about change, and some of the approaches that have previously found success.

Chapter 2 features Andrew Hedley, director of Hedley Consulting LTD, discussing the importance for an organization to become "change-able", having the means to adapt to new circumstances and situations. The chapter then moves into highlighting the key components of a successful change program, including developing the vision and strategy and communicating the process to the workforce.

In Chapter 3 Neryl East , writer, academic, speaker, and communication specalist, provides a framework for implementing successful change initiatives within an organization, outlining a number of well-known change management theories and processes – including McKinsey's 7-S model and Kotter's eight step process.

Chapter 4 features Duncan Hart, director of Duncan Hart Consulting, discussing the process of resourcing and supporting an initiative made to address an opportunity for effective change. The chapter outlines a "stage-gate" approach, a multi-stage process for implementing change that allows for careful consideration and evaluation at every step. The chapter then moves to outline leaderships role in utilizing the "stage-gate" process.

Chapter 5 features Carol Mynott, director at PWC, exploring the need for proper succession planning to ensure that the loss of a partner does not mean the loss of a client. The steps that a firm can take to future proof themselves are run through, such as rethinking the renumeration process and ensuring open and honest communication.

Chapter 6 features Arthur Greene, principal at Boyer Greene LLC, discussing the best ways to encourage a shift in behavior through modifying the partner compensation system. The methods of establishing which behaviors are preferred are outlined, and how best to introduce a new compensation system that incentivizes them.

In Chapter 7 Nick Marson, CEO of The Parallel Mind, explains the neuroscience behind change management, and how leadership can use an understanding of this to help garner a smooth transition in partners – by utilizing empathy and emotional intelligence to foster and build relationships.

Chapter 8 features Bob Murray and Alicia Fortinberry, principals at Fortinberry Murray, discussing the best methods for getting a commitment to change with a workforce, outlining some of the reasons why individuals attempt to resist change, and how to overcome the resistance to lead to a transformation that stays with the organization.

And finally in Chapter 9 Patrick J. McKenna, author, lecturer, strategist, and advisor to premier law firms, discusses the best strategic approaches to introducing change within a law firm. Answering questions on why change is so difficult for firms, and what some of the major hurdles that can be found during periods of transition, Patrick summarizes the state of change management for firms and runs through some of best approaches and leadership styles to succeed.

With disruption in legal services predicted to continue for some time, it will be those firms who adapt, put into place, and act upon a change management strategy that will be the ones who capitalize on the changes to come.

# About the authors

**Neryl East**, MA, PhD, is a writer, academic, speaker, and communication specialist with extensive experience in both internal and external communication in Australian government, private sector, and not-for-profit organizations. Neryl's specialties include issues management, change management, and integrating new and traditional media. She lectures in public relations and journalism, is in demand as a keynote presenter and trains organizations in many facets of communication including media skills and writing in plain language. In 2010 Neryl was selected as an ambassador for the Year of Women in Local Government, a programme supported by the Australian government. She is a member of the Public Relations Institute of Australia and the National Speakers Association of Australia. Neryl is the author of *Named and Shamed*, Rod Oxley's inside story of the Wollongong corruption scandal and the ARK Group's *Strategic Internal Communications for Complex Organizations* report, now in its second edition. Neryl can be contacted via her website.

**Alicia Fortinberry**, PhD (Organizational Psychology) has gained international recognition over two decades for her powerful, lasting impact on organizations and leaders globally. Alicia enables organizations to build the leadership, performance, and culture that will achieve their vision and strategy. In addition to her work as a consultant, facilitator, and high-level executive coach, Alicia is a best-selling author and keynote speaker. She combines a clear, engaging, and practical communication style with a proven evidence-based approach and strategic acumen.

With her highly experienced and credentialed Fortinberry Murray team, Alicia works with organizations and governments globally to help leaders shape and implement winning strategies using research-based understanding of human motivation and change.

With her colleague Dr Bob Murray, Alicia won the American Science Achievement Award (2012) and has been appointed to head the US government's comprehensive national work stress initiative. Alicia's pioneering work is backed by the latest research in neuroscience, genetics, and management. Together with Bob, she has presented her work at leading universities such as Duke, Tufts, California State, and Sydney University.

With Bob she authored the international best-selling books *Creating Optimism*, *Raising an Optimistic Child* (both McGraw-Hill), which have become standards in the fields of optimism and resilience. Most recently Alica and Bob published *Leading the Future: The Human Science of Law Firm Strategy and Leadership* (ARK Group, 2016).

Alicia received her Masters in Psychology and Journalism from Columbia University and her PhD in Organizational Psychology from the University of Phoenix. She is a member of the American Psychological Association, the American Association for the Advancement of Science, and the American Society of Journalists and Authors.

**Arthur G. Greene** is a principal with Boyer Greene LLC, a law firm consulting firm with offices in Ann Arbor, MI and Bedford, NH (www.boyergreene.com). Following a successful career as a practicing lawyer, during which he served as managing partner of a firm that grew to 70 lawyers, Arthur has turned his professional focus to management consulting with law firms. In recent years, his consulting practice has included profitability studies, revenue enhancement, firm audits, strategic planning, governance, succession planning, mergers and acquisitions, compensation plans, alternative billing methods, and other aspects of maintaining a healthy firm.

He has lectured, conducted workshops, and authored articles and books on a variety of law firm issues. His recent ABA books, *The Lawyer's Guide to Governance* and *The Lawyer's Guide to Increasing Revenue*, are both in their second edition. His most recent book, *Arthur Greene's Practical Guide: Succession Plans for Law Firms and Rewards for Retiring Lawyers*, is found at www.arthurggreene.com. Arthur is a longstanding member of the American Bar Association and has served as chair of its Law Practice Management Section. He is also a fellow of the College of Law Practice Management. Arthur can be reached at agg@arthurggreene.com.

**Duncan Hart** practiced as a barrister and solicitor for over 20 years before becoming the regional managing director of one of Australasia's largest firms with over 2,000 employees. He became a full-time consultant in 2002. His various consultancies have taken him from Silicon Valley to Shanghai, and his clients include not only law firms, but a wide cross-section of industry groups, including manufacturing, health, education, and IT.

Duncan's first book, *The Strategic Law Firm* (Ark Group, 2010), argued the case for a more strategic approach to law firm management, and in particular the adoption of the types of strategic planning tools and methodologies that he had seen in operation in many of his clients' industry sectors.

More recently, his background in intellectual property has led him to explore more closely the role of disruptive technologies and business models in various sectors, including law, patent attorney, and other professions. Many of his recent assignments involve the so called "start-up" sector, and larger more mature industries where clients are seeking to develop innovation-based strategies in fields as diverse as bio-tech and logistics.

In all his assignments, Duncan draws from a rich palette of industry and professional experience, and he is committed to the belief that law firms, like any other businesses, have much to learn from other sectors, particularly in the area of innovation-based strategy. In short, they should be encouraged to experiment to find new, and hopefully better, solutions for both the firm and their clients.

**Andrew Hedley** helps the leaders of law firms to create mold-breaking strategies, develop strong brands, forge robust client relationships, and design compelling propositions. In addition to his strategic project advice, Andrew is much sought after as a strategy group guide, partner retreat speaker, workshop facilitator, and moderator. He is a respected contributor to specialist strategy and management publications and a regular keynote conference speaker. He is the author of three ARK Group publications: *The Law Firm Merger: A Leader's Guide to Strategy & Realisation* (2014), *Client Strategy in a Changing Legal Market* (2011), and *Developing Strategic Client Relationships* (2008).

Following his MA, Andrew completed an MBA in 1993. Both focused on professional services strategy and business development. He has approaching 25 years' experience of managing and advising professional service firms, with more than 15 years focused on the legal sector, prior to which he was the managing director of an architectural practice. He was the business development director of two leading international law firms for nine years before establishing Hedley Consulting in 2005.

Andrew is a member of the Advisory Panel of NetworkMP, a leading peer network for managing partners of professional service firms. He sits on the judging panel of the MPF European Practice Management Awards and The Lawyer Management Awards. He is the course director of the Cambridge Marketing College CIM Professional Diploma in Professional Services Marketing, the only CIM accredited qualification focused on the needs of the professional services sector.

Andrew has been admitted as a fellow of the Institute of Directors, the Strategic Planning Society, the Chartered Management Institute, Cambridge Marketing College, and the Royal Society of Art. He can be contacted at: andrew.hedley@hedleyconsulting.com. For more information, see: www.hedleyconsulting.com.

**Nick Marson** is the founder of The Parallel Mind Ltd, which coaches CEOs and senior executives of professional services firms to help them find their authentic voice and deliver their message effectively. His clients range across the banking, insurance, and legal sectors; including Allianz, Deutsche Bank, J P Morgan, Baker McKenzie, Clifford Chance, Hogan Lovells, and Linklaters.

Previously, Nick's background was in insurance (FCII/CIP) and financial services. He held senior management roles with the Royal Insurance Group and Standard Chartered Bank where he was responsible for Insurance products, and ran a tied agency for the Bank's Legal and General Financial Planning service.

Nick is an ICF advanced level executive coach having graduated at the Academy of Executive Coaching, and ran a major research project for the CII in conjunction with CASS Business School City University London looking at the link between top leadership behaviour and innovative organizations.

**Patrick J. McKenna** is an internationally recognized author, lecturer, strategist, and seasoned advisor to the leaders of premier law firms; having had the honor of working with at least one of the largest firms in over a dozen different countries.

He is the author of eight books most notably his international business best seller, *First Among Equals*, currently in its sixth printing and translated into nine languages. His most recent work, *The Changing of the Guard, Second Expanded Edition* (ARK Group, 2017), provides in-depth guidance on the leadership selection process in professional firms and resulted in his being acknowledged in *American Lawyer* magazine as "a longtime succession consultant and coach to new firm leaders."

Patrick's three decades of experience led to his being the subject of a Harvard Law School Case Study entitled *Innovations In Legal Consulting* (2011). One example of that innovation was his launching the first instructional program designed to specifically address the issues that new firm leaders of larger firms face in their First 100 Days – which has thus far graduated over 80 new leaders many from AmLaw 100 and 200-sized law firms, as well as from notable accounting and consulting firms.

Patrick serves as contributing editor to *Of Counsel*, The Legal Practice and Management Report based in New York City; writes a monthly thought leadership column for *Legal Executive Institute*; is the only expert in professional service firms admitted to the Association of Corporate Executive Coaches, the #1 US group for senior-level CEO coaches; and is the recipient of an honorary fellowship from Leaders Excellence of Harvard Square (2015).

Patrick may be reached at: patrick@patrickmckenna.com.

**Bob Murray**, MBA, PhD (Clinical Psychology), is an internationally recognized expert in strategy, leadership, human personality, and behavioral change. Distinguished for his ability to uncover the core of issues, Bob has developed ground-breaking methods for measuring, benchmarking, and improving an organization's capacity for change and adaptation.

Bob's insights are based on his wide experience and also on his deep knowledge of research in the areas of management, psychology, genetics, and neurobiology. Clients include premier law firms such as Allens Linklaters, Ashurst, and Herbert Smith Freehills; and other top tier companies such as KPMG, Macquarie Bank, PwC, Ford, Caterpillar, McDonald's, PepsiCo, BHP, Wesfarmers, and Stockland.

Bob is an acclaimed keynote speaker and is widely published. With Dr Alicia Fortinberry, Bob received the American Science Achievement Award (2012) and advises the US government on workplace stress and other workplace issues. He specializes in ensuring executive teams develop and drive strategies that will be embraced and actioned.

Bob's previous experience includes working for Hill Samuel Merchant Bank, where he helped to turn around distressed companies, as well working as a BBC producer. With Alicia, he authored the best-selling books *Creating Optimism* and *Raising an Optimistic Child* (McGraw-Hill). These international best-sellers have become standards in the fields of optimism and resilience.

Bob has lectured at Sydney, Duke, Tufts, South Florida, and California State universities. He received his MBA from Sydney University (where he also earned his MA in Psychology) and his PhD from New York University.

Bob is a member of the American Psychological Association, the American Association for the Advancement of Science, and the American Society of Journalists and Authors.

**Carol Mynott** is a director within PWC's HRS practice, specialising in global mobility and HR consulting to the legal sector, having worked with firms for the last eight years. She works with a number of international law firms, advising on their global mobility frameworks and is responsible for the global coordination of their expatriate tax compliance.

**David J. Parnell** is an author, speaker, *Forbes* and *American Lawyer* Media columnist, and the founder and principal of True North Partner Management, a partner-level legal search and placement firm. Along with his experience in private placement, he has previously worked in-house with the likes of Intel, Xircom, and DreamWorks SKG. Complimenting his *Forbes* and *ALM* columns, his work can also be found in publications such as *The American Lawyer*, the *Huffington Post*, *Venture Capital Post*, *Fox News Magazine*, *Lawyerist*, *Law360*, *Bloomberg*, *Australasian Lawyer*, *NBC News*, the *Global Legal Post*, *Business Insider*, and *NZ Lawyer*, among others.

# Chapter 1: Understanding change – Understanding and working with the legal mind

*By David J. Parnell, founder and principal of True North Partner Management*

## Why do many lawyers find change to be so difficult?

In a word: control.

The fact that lawyers are generally controlling by nature won't be a surprise to you. Whether that tendency is nature or nurture or both is still up for debate – it's likely both – but to really understand why this is such a challenge for law firms looking to initiate change, follow along with me for a moment as we take a look at the underlying biology and psychology that generates and governs this.

### Predictability at the synaptic level

To effectively navigate life, our minds generate "schemas", which are mental maps or models of our environment, how things in our environment work, and the best way to navigate them. This includes everything you do and interact with, from brushing your teeth to making your significant other laugh to ordering lunch to arguing in front of a judge. And while much goes into creating these schemas from a biological and psychological perspective, one of the most important neurological processes is known as dopamine reward prediction error coding; a crucial element for basic learning.[1]

It works like this: Imagine that you are a kid again, it's Saturday morning and you are getting ready to pour yourself a bowl of cereal. If things go as planned – you pour the cereal and milk, eat it, it tastes delicious, and you are on your way – i.e., your *predictions* of the event based on your "cereal for breakfast" schema are met – your dopamine remains at baseline, resulting in, basically, nothing: the status quo. Now imagine that you don't expect to find a toy in this type of cereal, but this time one fell out while you poured it. Here, your schema's *prediction* is met with a pleasant surprise, and as a result, more dopamine is released than normal, a good feeling follows, and a new lesson is learned: this is your new favorite cereal. On the other hand, let's say that you actually expected a toy to be in the cereal – i.e., your schema *predicted* that one would be present – but it ultimately wasn't. Here, a negative surprise happens and the dopamine released falls well below your baseline, a bad feeling follows, and again, a lesson is learned: "I hate this cereal." The error in the schema's prediction is used to make judgments, and "learning" comes in the form of strengthened neuronal pathways which turn into beliefs, knowledge, habits, and other forms of "data" that are used to strengthen and/or modify existing, and develop new, schemas.

Now, important to our discussion are the notions that (i) "prediction" is a key *fundamental* aspect of our neurology and psychology, and (ii) our brain pays attention to *difference* in our environment based on that prediction, i.e., that which *does not* fit into a given schema rather than that which does. Think about it: if your brain paid attention to everything that it already *knows*, it would quickly overload. Just look at the room you are in right now. When you walked into it, did you consciously register and consider the door, the door hinges, the door knob, the trim around the door, the design of the door, the type of flooring, the color of the walls, the texture of the walls, the type of light in the room, the number of lights in the room? The list goes on, and on, and on... Your mind builds schemas that can make snap judgements on all of these things so that you can just get on with life. And it is only when something doesn't fit into that schema – i.e., it doesn't fit your predictions – that it hits your radar so as to modify your schema for future prediction.

### Evolution and environmental stressors

Now, take this type of learning system and run it through millions of years of evolution in an environment that is hostile, has no medical care, little food or shelter, poses almost ridiculous levels of competition, and provides near constant danger. A few things happen, here:

First, with little access to consistent food sources we generally create schemas consisting of beliefs, habits, and "methods of operation" that require the least amount of effort to accomplish a given task. This is where the principle of least effort (or Zipf's Law from Harvard Linguist George Kingsley Zipf) derives from. Second, where danger is plentiful and the stakes are super high if one is hurt – remember, a simple cut can actually kill you from infection – our brain pays much more attention to, and is more strongly motivated by, *negative* differences, and learns negative lessons more vividly (due also in part to the highly potent amygdaloid complex playing a crucial role in creating fear memory and modulating stress-induced emotional responses).[2] Lastly, where we do not have schemas in place – in other words, we have no knowledge of a situation – we have no way of predicting an outcome, which is highly uncomfortable for us. "I don't know what is in that dark cave, and frankly, I don't want to find out…"

So, what am I getting at here? Well, if we have a brain that automatically and subconsciously spends more time looking out for danger than opportunities, seeks efficiency as a top priority, and desires predictability because it hates the unknown, what commodity would be of the highest value to it? Control.

If you mull this over for just a second, I think you'll find that complete control over one's environment is as predictable, efficient, and safe as it gets. And the goal of achieving this – though driven at a very fundamental, subconscious level – plays out today in various instinctual, subconsciously driven and automatic processes, heuristics, and biases. For instance:

- We exhibit a strong status quo bias which predisposes us to disproportionately stick with the status quo as opposed to moving into the unknown.[3]
- Consider fear of the dark. Manifest in most children and adults (but to a lesser degree, but still present) is instinctual rather than learned, and based on an inability to predict what may come from the dark. To quote Dr. William E Lyons, author of Cambridge University Press' Emotion: "Fear of the dark may not be fear of the absence of light but fear of the absence of knowledge or, to put it more exactly, fear arising because one does not know what might be out there in the dark …"[4]
- We generally exhibit what is known as a negativity bias, which refers to the phenomenon that when we are posed with equally pleasant and unpleasant options, the unpleasant option will have a greater effect on our mental state. Colloquially, we respond more intensely to the whip rather than the carrot.[5]
- Our negativity bias dove tails into loss aversion, which, in psychologist and Nobel Prize winner Daniel Kahneman's words means that "losses loom larger than gains." This is a subset of Kahneman and (Amos) Tversky's prospect theory, which in a nutshell states that people make decisions based on the potential

value of losses and gains rather than the final outcome, and that people evaluate these losses and gains using certain heuristics. This leads to biases such as risk aversion, loss aversion, and people often preferring the status quo – "the devil they know."[6]

- Cognitive dissonance – the state of having inconsistent thoughts, beliefs, or attitudes, especially as relating to behavioral decisions and attitude change – is highly uncomfortable. And if you boil this down, the inconsistency is in essence a lack of predictability: a path has not been chosen, so we are in limbo and can't make informed decisions.[7]
- We are social by nature, and this drive for socialization has its roots in accessing resources that help to better control our environment and provide safety.[8]
- From our anthropological perspective, cultures – which comprise systems, processes, beliefs, methods, etc., that have proven to be effective for manipulating and controlling an environment – manifest for the explicit purpose of providing predictability through control of a group's environment.[9a, 9b]

### What our career says about us

These are but a handful of examples whereby our drive for predictability, safety, and control play out in the real world; there are reams of other data on this. And admittedly, much of this may sound like I am implying a lack of volition – free will. While that's a discussion for another day, it is difficult to dispute the realities listed above, so let's work with them because they do provide a useful lens through which to assess change in the law firm. So, with this considerable evidence pointing toward a drive for predictability and control over our environment, what can be gleaned from looking at our day to day behavior? More specifically, how about from looking at our careers?

Careers provide myriad things – fulfillment, challenge, friends, entertainment, esteem, self-value, etc. – but by far the most important earned resource from a career is capital – financial, social, reputational, etc. – which is used to directly or indirectly provide security, food, shelter, education, and just about everything that is necessary to live. The entrepreneur, the stone mason, the bus driver, the mechanic, the lawyer, they have all chosen those professions because, based on the combination of their knowledge, exposure to options and situations, experience, networks, access to opportunities, etc., their career path was their best choice for providing them with a tool to effectuate some level of *control* over their environment. To be direct, our schemas, our beliefs, our values, our personalities, and more are tools and methods learned through observation and trial and error about how best to navigate, compete in, extract resources from, and create predictability in our environment. Certainly, at a fundamental psychological level our careers and the networks that we build are tools, the purpose of which is instituting some level of control over our environment (we'll discuss this more in-depth in the next section on cultures).

Now let's get more specific about the legal industry. If you really think deeper about best practices for effectuating control over something, certainly understanding the rules by which the control target functions is the best place to start. Seeking to work with – to control – chemicals? Learn the laws of chemistry. Seeking to defy gravity? Learn the physics of flight. I think you get my point. If you have the "user's manual" to your target, you can figure it out! Now, through that lens, consider the purpose of the law. It is the very rule book by which a modern, civilized society works. And to most effectively work within, and if necessary, manipulate and control a situation within that society to best of one's ability, those who know, and can effectively and efficiently work within the rules, are going to have a distinct advantage, full stop. Where, even just a thousand years ago, size and strength used to be the most important tools for competition, dominance, and survival, today it is knowledge, and knowledge of the rules, that govern society and professional and social order in particular. And to effectively use and manipulate the knowledge that governs one's environment – the law – is to maximize one's potential for *controlling* that environment.

The legally-inclined mind – i.e., the psychology that sets one on the path to become a lawyer in the first place – is the alpha-control mind. This mind is driven to acquire and make useable the most powerful force for control that the civilized world offers. A bit dramatic? Maybe. But true, nevertheless? I say yes. If you consider the ever-present fundamental aspects that drive us to be efficient, risk averse, and to seek predictability through control, these *must* loom even larger in the mind of an attorney, whether by nature or nurture or a combination of the two. And acquiring those legal tools and skills gained on the path to learning jurisprudence – decisiveness, logic, rationale, etc. – that alpha-control mind is armed with an arsenal that serves to reinforce, and more effectively act upon, its pre-existing affinities.

The career of an attorney, in particular, is built upon a platform of control and predictability, both of which are the enemy of change. This begets the question: how can leadership inch this type of psychology toward the acceptance of change initiatives?

## Understanding the hurdles to bringing about change

### Motivating the firm

Configuration Theory concerns itself with the relationship between the design of an organization, its people, and the way that the firm functions and evolves as a result. Importantly, the theory recognizes that as cultures, norms, policies, procedures, and day-to-day routines take hold, inertia sets in – particularly when the organization is successful. To break this inertia – as both physics and management studies tell us[10a, 10b] – significant energy is necessary to get the organization mobilized toward a new direction. To better understand, let's consider how specifically a given configuration develops and ultimately evolves.

Strategic management professors Royston Greenwood and Bob Hinings argue that the dynamic of power relations within the organization, and the evolving pattern of commitments to existing and alternative interpretive schemes, as much as the alignment of internal and external contingencies, influence the organization-specific pattern of evolution toward a particular archetype. They call this path an organizational track. For the moment, let it be known that an organization's psychology (culture) will generate interpretive schemes that deem "best practices," as they pertain to remaining competitive within their (current) environment. These interpretive schemes combine into a structure that supports, incentivizes, facilitates, and governs those best practices; this is a firm's governance model. And as the internal and external environment shifts – which they both inevitably do – the dynamic between their interactions dictates the ongoing "best" practices for the (then) current environment (as it pertains to remaining competitive). With this in mind, if you look at an organization's "timeline" from its inception to-date, you will see a particular path it has followed – this is its track.

### Change isn't easy...

So, if that is how a firm's initial configuration comes to be, how do complete configurational shifts occur as they plod along their evolutionary track? Obviously, none of today's goliath firms started out with their current structure. They grew and matured and went through growth spurts, if you will. And these spurts take a certain alignment of planets, or better stated, a perfect storm to spur them along.

In remaining with the holistic approach, Configuration Theory recognizes that organizations, like any other organism or community, succumb to inertial forces. Cultures, norms, policies, procedures, and any other repetitive and consistent day-to-day events become routine, comfortable and otherwise, easy. As such, the mobilization of significant amounts of energy and effort are required to "move", or evolve from one archetype to another. This might be likened to a buildup of energy or emotion in a person. If you anger them once, they shrug it off. If you anger them twice, it may not be as easy to let go. If you anger them three times, however, they just might blow their lid… Though the concept of an organization may seem quite static, concrete, and non-human, studies, observations, and anecdotal evidence proves them to be quite dynamic and "human", indeed.

In their book, *Organizations: A Quantum View* (1984), Danny Miller, Peter H. Friesen, and Henry Mintzberg argue that radical change (as opposed to slow, linear, and methodical change) is not only necessary to break the powerful forces of inertia, but also minimizes the risk of organizational incoherence during the transition, thereby reducing the (unavoidable) costs incurred. Building on the concept of Configuration Theory, they distinguish two types of change periods: (i) momentum, which is defined as a long period of incremental adjustments that maintain or reinforce the existing configuration, and (ii) revolution, which is defined as a rare and short period of extensive and abrupt movement that gives rise to a new configuration. This line of reasoning is (also) pursued by Michael Tushman (Chair of Harvard's Program for Leadership Development) and Elaine Romanelli (business professor at Georgetown), who propose a "punctuated equilibrium" framework of organizational change; they elaborate on Miller, Friesen, and Mintzberg's main insights by articulating the dynamics characterizing equilibrium periods (relatively long periods of stability, i.e., momentum) and revolutionary periods (abrupt changes, i.e., revolution).

Another opinion is that of Greenwood, Hinings, et al., who characterize the movement between archetypes as sequences of interpretive decoupling and recoupling. Inherent to their theory is the co-existence of varied and conflicting archetypical criteria and components within any organization that serve to create a form of organizational cognitive dissonance (and therefore, internal conflict) that eventually leads to change and archetypal incoherence. This notion in particular fit's quite nicely with the cultural-based, bottom up theory of archetypical emergence. Any firm or organization does indeed derive from, and support, a prevailing psychology that dictates the firm's structure and activities – this is irrefutable. And much like the motivating discomfort that cognitive dissonance creates in an individual's psychology, cultural (group) psychology can experience the same type of dissonance and ultimately be motivated to move to a new organizational "stage" in an attempt to remedy the issues. As you may imagine, this transition is usually not without difficulties, however.

Attempts to remedy an ongoing crisis can be negated or reversed if and when established power relationships are mobilized to secure the status quo. As a result, efforts to evolve may be aborted, creating "non-linear tracks" or reversals in an organization's time line. So, rather than seeing organizations following a more linear, generic cycle of momentum followed by revolution that is led by a visionary leader, Greenwood and Hinings suggest that movement between archetypes can best be described as following varied and in some cases, even abrupt, non-linear paths. Apart from the dominant track of inertia, this can include a range of possible tracks – linear, oscillating, delayed, abortive, unresolved, etc., all of which are attempts at reorientation toward a more effective structure, with a successful reorientation being defined as achievement of archetypal coherence.

Ultimately, the history of most organizations will consist of extended periods of gradual growth that are connected by brief periods of dramatic change. In the legal realm, these theories are certainly realities. Almost all of the firms I studied attempted dramatic change – usually in the form of a merger – but only in the eleventh hour and once they were bathed in a critical mass of discomfort and desperation. The result for all of them was a major reversal that consisted of dissolution or bankruptcy. This is quite important, as these attempts at structural change are literally one of the points at which a firm will sink or swim.[11]

In summation, most major change initiatives are born from intense dissonance and discomfort within the firm. This creates its own set of challenges, and thus begets the questions: how can leadership (i) consider change during times of prosperity rather than famine? And (ii) how can leadership gain buy-in from the partnership when the status quo is *actually* attractive?

## Movement without spooking the herd

The standing cycle of change in the legal industry has created a tenuous situation for those firms seeking to implement a change initiative. Consider the following:

A firm begins the process of a major change – say, revamping its compensation model. Certainly, there will be some portion of the partnership that is unhappy with the effort. The comfort of the devil one knows – the status quo – is usually attractive; certainly, for those that are benefiting most from the current state of affairs change will be unwelcome and potentially even a non-starter. As is always the case (with major firms) the initiative is leaked to the public and ultimately the press; the protection of sources guaranteeing sources' anonymity ensures this.

Now, whether the initiative comes from a position of strength or weakness matters not. The press, as it usually does, turns the initiatives into a weakness for the firm. In fact, this has happened so many times over the years that even if the press doesn't take a negative angle on it, the readership generally will, anyway. As you can imagine, this causes concern, paranoia, even dissent within the firm. The partnership wants to trust leadership, and often times they do, and if it were left there, things may eventually just level out. But usually it isn't left there, as clients see this in the news, the durability of the firm is drawn into question, rainmakers are made aware of clients' concerns and despite the client manager's best efforts to calm concerned parties, the clients threaten to move business elsewhere with or without their handlers.

Is this scenario exaggerated? Along with other partners who have been materially injured by the new compensation model, often enough a portion of the firm ultimately leaves due to client threats, a general lack of information, or even misinformation swirling in the public eye. Whether the amount of departures is material enough to cause real damage may be another story, but the departures happen nevertheless.

This cycle reinforces the reality that most change initiatives are, in actuality, catalyzed by *materially* negative events. In other words, it usually takes a large *whip* to catalyze movement, not a large carrot. Most leadership understands the danger of announcing change, more often than not leaving them to institute major change as a last resort. Rare is the firm that makes material change initiatives from a position of strength. As a result, the market has been conditioned – clients and attorneys alike – to see change as a red flag, a problem, a potential collapse waiting to happen, regardless of its catalyst.

This begets the question: how can leadership institute change while avoiding the damaging and potentially catalyzing optics?

## The overall cohesiveness of the firm

The term "culture" is used so often in the industry that it has become a buzz word. To most, "culture" is the personality of the firm. And when they inquire about it, they are often really asking "what is it like working there?" But a firm's culture represents much more than just a personality or an experience. Culture comprises beliefs, values, assumptions, dress, proprietary technology, addresses, firm-focused social and professional norms, jargon, and much more. There are a lot of ingredients that go into a firm's culture that move like shadows below radar.

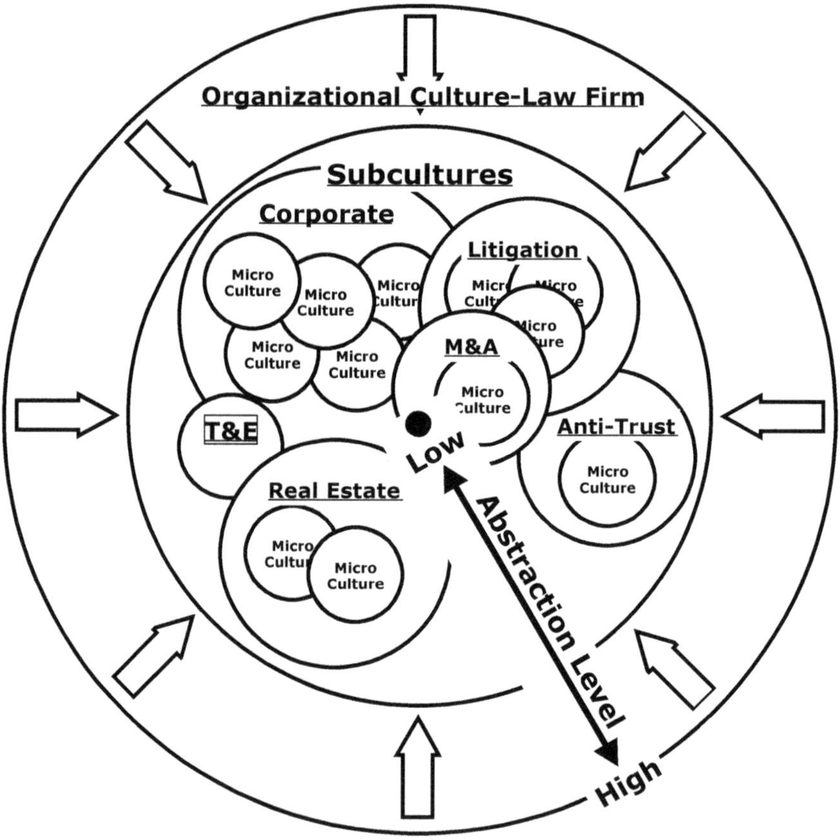


*Figure 1: Macro-culture*[12]

Cultures arise out of a group's need to effectively survive and compete in its respective environment. And the methods of operation, beliefs, values, habits, strategies, etc. that ultimately take hold, and from which the culture is built, are selected as a direct result of the pressures and stressors that are unique to the group's situation. This is an important point, as unique "environments" arise in the darnedest of places, including *within* an established culture. This creates the reality that if an organization is large enough, its culture becomes stratified, supporting sub- and micro-cultures.

- In a stratified cultutral setting, there are higher, more abstract and diffused layers of culture that govern and interact with, but also generally govern, lower, more concrete layers.
- Macro-culture – This is geographically based and is the most abstract of the strata, influencing the most fundamental beliefs in the framework. Consider Eastern versus Western cultures.
- Organizational culture – In the real world, fragments of an organizational culture are often found in mission statements, visions, goals, etc., and where law firms are concerned this is often publicly labeled with terms such as small firm, large firm, European firm, UK-based firm, international firm, sweatshop firm, white shoe firm, collegial firm, lifestyle firm, elitist firm, boutique firm, etc.
- Sub- and micro-cultures – Sub-cultures often arise from practice areas, specific geographies, floors of a building, etc. Micro-cultures often manifest as fiefdoms within an office.

Because cultures – whether macro-, organizational-, sub-, or micro- – arise as behaviors and rule sets that are unique to a given environment, as you can imagine, the sub-culture of a labor and employment group in Knoxville, TN, will be different than that of a finance group in Manhattan. Different rules and different traits are successful in each respective area/practice. This means that a materially sized firm doesn't necessarily have a singular "culture" per se, but an amalgamation of many sub- and micro-cultures that, in their interactions, help create and define the organizational culture. At the same time, the organizational culture directly influences, at a very fundamental level, the composition of those sub- and micro-cultures. The layers are integrated and reciprocally influential. And the way that these sub- and micro-cultures interact on the ground, in real time, is what Prof. Stephen Mayson might call a firm's "normative environment", which is, basically, how things *actually* happen, versus how they are supposed to happen – there is often a difference. As a simple example, a firm may purport that it is "collaborative", but when you drill down it simply isn't. Where this phenomenon poses challenges to firms looking to begin a change initiative:

1. On the less extreme end, sub- and micro-cultures can be somewhat removed from the firm's overall center of gravity, making it more difficult to rally them to action.
2. On the more extreme end, sub- and micro-cultures can turn "counter" and become factions, balkanizing the firm. In this case, depending on the influence of the faction/s, it can become impossible for a firm to effectively rally the majority of the firm to deploy change. In a worst-case scenario, the initiative itself can become the catalyst for sending one or more factions on their way.
3. In creating strategy, which is often where change initiatives begin, it is difficult to make one that is suitable, acceptable, and feasible – three criteria necessary for effective strategy development – without having a thorough understanding of all of the needs, interests, and realities of the power sources within your firm. And to do this, it is necessary to understand your firm's cultural composition.[13]

This begets the questions: (i) Does leadership understand the composition of their firm's materially influential sub- and micro-cultures? And (ii) how can leadership cohere and motivate the various groups within the firm?

## What definitely does not work in introducing change

### Fiat

This is perhaps the greatest challenge to law firm leadership that is seeking to induce change: fiat is not an option. If you look at the corporate realm, the CEO has significantly more authority and tools to induce change. They own the "product"; mission-critical positions or employees are rare; fiat can be invoked if necessary, and the simple understanding by employees that it is on the table as an option usually means it isn't necessary to call into play. This is not unlike a cold war.

Where law firms are concerned, however – and I know that this is been said a million times before – the "books of business" that are the very lifeblood of the law firm *have options* and thus can leave if it suits them. Fiat doesn't work in this environment, necessitating significantly more tact and consensus if change is going to be effective. This takes time, resources, and bandwidth that is often in short supply.

So, you will need to take into account a very conservative estimate of the time, resources, and political capital that are necessary to effectively institute the change. And if it something that will need to be driven hard rather than simply fostered, the risk is increased dramatically and warrants consideration.

**Leadership of the firm selling from a position of weakness**

In writing *The Failing Law Firm* I found a number of firms where law firm leadership just didn't have the support of the firm. This is an interesting concept as leadership is voted in by the partnership, which often leads leadership to believe that they're in a position of strength – rightfully so, as after all, they were voted in. That said, I know from study and experience that even leadership that is voted in may not have the respect and following of the firm as a whole.

Importantly, law firm governance is not the same as corporate governance, which goes much further toward inoculating against cronyism and politically influenced distributions of power, both of which still occur often enough. Professional rules prevent law firm governance from creating an effective separation of power and interests, and as a result, leadership is left vulnerable to any number of possible contaminations.

So, in short, the following of the majority is not a given, and needs to be heavily evaluated prior to considering a major change initiative.

**Change that is introduced on a balkanized platform**

Any law firm can, and often does, have a stratified culture. And in a firm that is financially and strategically healthy and has a strong, homogenous base of fundamental beliefs, values, and assumptions – i.e., a homogenous organizational culture – the (relatively minor) diversification is a strength. But where sub- and micro-cultures are counter *and* wield heavy influence within the firm, they can severely disrupt change efforts, sometimes by leaving. And departures during change initiatives hinder progress by (i) creating a lack of confidence in leadership and the initiative, potentially creating more dissention within the firm (which is generally due to the partnership's ignorance toward the actual circumstances that surround the departures), and (ii) drawing the eyes of the press which inherently fuels client concerns, potentially impacting revenue and incentivizing client handlers to leave.

So, if your firm is balkanized, change initiatives will quite necessarily need to be deployed very slowly, and should be geared toward bringing the firm together, first, and then taking on the long-term change initiative, second.

## Developing a sense of urgency that gets partner's attention

### Change initiatives need to be "sold," not just "marketed"

In order to properly package the need for change, it must be positioned *uniquely* with respect to the various groups that will experience the change. Think about it: a complete overhaul of your strategy will likely affect aging baby boomers much more differently than millennials. Likewise, if your headquarters is in New York and you have several satellite offices that don't have a critical mass, the satellites may feel very vulnerable regardless of what is said. This is important, because drawing distinctions between various groups and subgroups creates the map by which sales can begin to replace marketing.

Consider (at a higher level) the process of getting a consumer to *purchase* a car. Not consider a purchase, or do some research on the purchase, but actually exchange money for the good. The manufacturer, of course, produces and airs commercials and other materials to make potential consumers aware of their cars. They build awareness, notoriety, and a brand. But, where the rubber meets the road – pardon the pun – is in localized commercials and on the showroom floor with sales people. This is the difference between marketing and sales, and is instructive regarding change initiatives. Where top firm leadership should be the channel through which higher-level notifications and instructions are provided to the firm – the "marketing" if you will – the actual "sales" of the initiative should be performed by sources of influence closer to their respective groups.

Which groups? Well, firms can be parsed by practice, geography, responsibility, attorney titles, cohorts, or any number of other ways. It's important to understand the composition of your firm – governance models often provide a good structure to start from – and in particular where the power sources reside. This way you are (i) tailoring the change initiative in a way that at least doesn't offend, and ideally benefits, the various power sources in the firm (books of business, politically connected and influential partners, respected alpha lawyers, etc.), and (ii) tailoring your messages in a way that is unique and most influential to the respective groups.

### Getting a third-party analysis of the firm

When Patton Boggs was making big changes so as to streamline prior to its merger in 2014 – which ultimately formed Squire Patton Boggs – then managing partner Ed Newberry knew that there was going to be a real challenge ahead. While he was in good standing and respected by the firm, bankruptcy was a real option at the time and there were whispers in the halls. So, to ensure that (i) the viability of the content of his messages was intact with the partnership, and (ii) his partners really understood what bankruptcy was going to entail, he and his top management team (TMT) brought in Al Togut of Togut Segal, a highly-respected law firm bankruptcy attorney, to give the partnership a third party (objective) and professional analysis of the state of the firm, and a view into the realities of declaring bankruptcy, which aren't pretty.

This point is important: often enough when change is being introduced, the "true" intentions of management and leadership can be suspect to the partnership at large. Aside from various cultural and procedural underpinnings that may create a suspicious environment within a firm – a culture of opacity, for instance – there has been enough publicly pronounced deception in failed firms to, frankly, poison the well for many others. And if the partnership doesn't believe in the content and/or intent of the message, no amount of convincing will bring that boat safely to shore. With that in mind, if leadership and management are able to present *truly* objective, third-party assessments of the challenges the firm faces and predictions of where the firm is heading, this can go a very long way towards mobilizing the firm as a whole, and best positioning leadership and management to exert influence as the process unfolds.

### Storytelling and history can be very helpful

If you've read *Thinking, Fast and Slow* by Daniel Kahneman, or any cognitive psychology text book written in the last 15 years for that matter, you'll know that we have two separate brain systems – "implicit" and "explicit" – and that they respond differently to various types of information. There is significant data supporting the notion that the most influential types of information are those which create emotion. We'll call this type of information "analog": metaphors, analogies, similes, storytelling, etc. While analog information is, well, fuzzier than its counterpart – "digital" types of information: logic, rationale, pragmatism, "if-then", "either-or", objectivism, etc. – it is often much more influential because it speaks more directly to areas of our brain that create emotion and feelings – the stuff of motivation. Numbers, facts, data and the such often fall flat – at least flatter – where mobilizing the hearts and minds of the troops is concerned. And while there are various qualities that go into good storytelling – which are beyond the scope of this chapter – please take away from this that any leader looking to motivate and mobilize their firm should incorporate "analog" types of information into their messages and learn how to tell a good story.

Likewise, history can not only offer you good stories to tell, but also provides you with objective, unbiased proof of the points that you are trying to convey. For example, as of the moment of this writing, the market for intellectual property boutiques is experiencing significant pressure from legal consumers who are increasingly moving toward full-service firms. In fact, the IP boutique Kenyon & Kenyon merged (recently) with Andrews Kurth in 2016 as a result of, and as an illustration of, this pressure. Now, if you are leading an IP boutique and you know your history, you can draw on the rash of IP boutiques that didn't respond effectively to the consolidating market and failed between 2002-2010 as a result; e.g., Darby & Darby; Lyon & Lyon; Morgan & Finnegan, Skjervan Morrill, and Pennie & Edmonds. These would make powerful historic lessons and provide story fodder to rally, cohere, and mobilize the troops.

### Burning the boats

If you have all of your ducks in a row as you institute the change – i.e., the firm is cohesive, you have a quality strategy that is suitable, acceptable, and feasible, your strategy/change initiative is congruent with the various cultural underpinnings of the firm, you're confident that you have buy-in from the gross majority of the firm, etc. – then you "burn the boats".

For example, in an effort to become more competitive in an increasingly competitive environment, Kansas City, MO-based law firm Husch Blackwell decided to entirely change its infrastructure by adopting a fully sector-focused service portfolio. This was a fairly severe departure from the firm's traditional practice-focused composition, and the firm dived in head first, not allowing for any exceptions to the strategy. As you might imagine, there were some departures as a result, a learning curve, and some growing pains. But with effective planning, strategy development, third party consultation, and appropriate internal positioning, marketing, and sales of the effort, the partnership signed on for the ride, toughed out any challenges, and has come out on the other side an institution that has changed for the better.

While this may seem dramatic, it doesn't necessarily need to be carried out in such an extreme fashion to be effective. "Burning the boats" can take the form of *actively* enforcing the initiative and attaching compensation to its success or failure. In essence, you want to hold the firm's feet to the fire. And if someone doesn't hold up their responsibilities in due course, there needs to be repercussions for that, and the firm needs to know that those repercussions were administered. Obviously, it's important when you communicate this to the firm that it be done so in a constructive and non-dictatorial fashion, but the firm – or at least the partnership – should know that everyone is being held accountable.

## Some approaches that firm leaders have found to be effective

### Taking a long-term approach

Changing the course of a firm, just like that of a big ship, takes time. The firms that have successfully instituted change no doubt took their time, made sure that everything was done right, and approached it with an extended time horizon. You can't rush the development of the strategy; you can't rush or short change town hall meetings and soliciting feedback; you can't rush setting expectations effectively prior to deploying the change. The preparation process, in particular, is incredibly important not only from a practical standpoint – you want it done "right" rather than "right now" – but also from a signaling standpoint. If the firm sees that you've only put four weeks into your process, their confidence in the work product will suffer. Approach the initiative knowing that there will be an expanse of time where the forces of fear, uncertainty, and the process of acclimation will impose their will, potentially creating a challenging period on your firm's timeline – the "darkness" before the "dawn"

At the heart of this is instituting the change from a position of financial strength, as that strength provides a comfortable bunker in which to ride out the storm. Unfortunately, this is often not the position from which change comes about – see "Motivating the firm" above regarding Configuration Theory. Admittedly, there is a hidden benefit to a firm that is in distress: troubled times can cohere the firm as a whole, and the stress itself can act as the catalyzing agent to get the firm moving. You may have your qualms with an ex-spouse, for example, but if something is threatening a child you share with that spouse, see how quickly those qualms melt away as you band together and mobilize a unified front. At the same time if you get to choose which position that you'd like to institute change from – one of financial weakness or one of financial strength – you'd choose one of financial strength. And though reality often isn't so neat, strive to change from strength: i.e., change in the form of innovation, not desperation, and extend the "finish line" well into the future.

### Being inclusive of the gross majority of the firm

In 2011 Levi Strauss & Co. hired Chip Bergh as CEO to turn around the then financially struggling company. This was a big project, as at 160+ years old and one of the most iconic brands in the world, changing the course of public perception was a tall order. I interviewed Bergh for my *Forbes* column, and one of the most important aspects of their change initiative came in the form of company inclusiveness:

#### On rallying the troops to the LS&Co. cause

**Parnell**: How did you go about establishing employee loyalty to the company? To the brand? How did you go about cohering the company as a whole?

**Bergh**: Well, first of all, we had a pretty good starting point because the employees joined this company largely because of what the company stands for: Our values and our commitment to giving back to the communities where we live and work.

We have a concept called "profits through principles" which basically means the more earnings that we make and the more profits we deliver, the more we contribute back to the communities where we live and work. That goes all the way back to our founder, Levi Strauss, himself. The very first year he made a profit, he donated money back to the community here in San Francisco. So, we have very strongly rooted values, and I think that creates an incredible bond with our employees. We also have some of the world's most iconic brands. A lot of people work at this company because they love the Levi's® brand. It's part passion; and I like to say that passion is worth 10 index points.

So I think I had a pretty good starting point. But it was important to get people to recognize the reality of the situation: That the company really wasn't as successful as people believed it was, and that we had been very inconsistent in delivering results. And, clearly, a change in leadership at the C-level was a signal that there was dissatisfaction with the results the company had been delivering.

Then I put a strategy together with my executive team, and we worked to get people on board with what our key strategic choices were. And then to sustain it, I began doing monthly meetings that I call "Chips & Beer." They are basically town hall meetings held late in the afternoon, and we bring in beer for a one-hour Q&A session. I don't do canned PowerPoint presentations or anything. I give a three to five minute update on the state of the business, and then we open the floor up for questions. So, I do that every month when I'm in San Francisco at our home base. And when I travel, I always make a point of connecting with our employees in an open forum, question-and-answer-type of format or town hall meeting.

> We also have a full cascade through our leadership team. Although we are a privately held company, we hold a quarterly earnings call with analysts because we have publicly traded debt. We always follow the earnings call with a Q&A session with leaders. So, the people feel really connected and attached to the results. And they have an opportunity to see how their work connects back to the overall progress that we are making as a company.[14]

Actively engaging people in the change process is often integral to the success of it. Town hall meetings give leadership a chance to show their face in the various offices and exudes a true interest in receiving feedback. Where your firm is concerned, this means interacting with not only the partners, but also the associates and the administrative staff in some way. I don't think it's wise to underestimate the influence that these groups can have on the firm as a whole, even if we are just talking about information leakage to the media.

An illustration from the legal field is Steve Browne of Bingham McCutchen. While Bingham McCutchen might not be the best example for a successful change initiative, as the leader of a firm that found itself in extraordinary circumstances, Steve Brown did a *very* good job of interacting with the firm on the whole and gaining their loyalty during the firm's process of change, and we saw this in the exceedingly low information leakage to the media.

### Eating the elephant: Momentum

I'm sure you've heard the old saying about how one should eat an elephant: one bite at a time. Change in the firm is no different. It needs to be broken down into sufficiently small and proximal steps. This is not only important from a sheer logistical standpoint, but perhaps more importantly is that as each step is completed successfully, momentum builds.

Momentum and inertia are *exceedingly* consequential phenomena in the course of change. As we know from the section "Motivating the firm" above regarding Configuration Theory, to break inertia requires significant energy, and that energy comes in the form of momentum, and a great catalyst for momentum is momentum itself. It can't be understated how much momentum success can create – no matter how big or small the success. And aren't small successes much easier to achieve? At the same time, it can't be underestimated how patiently inertia can and will wait to take hold at the first sign of failure.

### Boiling the frog: Expectations

You've probably heard the term "boiling the frog." And while you may have even used it before, you've probably not researched the phrase. Studies have been conducted on boiling frogs – I know, I know, unbelievable; but true nevertheless – and as long as the temperature is turned up at a sufficiently slow rate, they don't jump out of the pot and eventually boil to death. And while one of the major themes from the boiled frog is to expose the firm to challenges slowly and methodically – see the section on "Taking a long-term approach" – another important theme is the concept of relativity.

212-degree water is really, really hot when compared to 90-degree water. But 91-degree water isn't a whole lot hotter than 90-degree water, and 92 from 91, and 93 from 92, and 94 from 93, and the next thing you know, your legs are being served with Creole dipping sauce in a restaurant. In other words, one's perception of an event/experience is a function of their expectations. As a result, how expectations are set – the relative point from which judgments will subsequently be made – dictates (at least to a material degree) the positivity or negativity of one's perception of the event/experience.

Putting this into functional terms, your firm will gauge the success and speed of your change initiative based on their expectations, and those expectations will (at least in part) be set by you. If those expectations are not met in some material way, the frogs will jump. This means that you can set the rules of relativity, as they relate to your initiative, by controlling expectations. "Bad" is a relative thing. If expectations are set correctly – this means no pie-in-the-sky goals, reasonable/achievable milestones are set, notification that possible/probable hurdles will appear in the future (the loss of laterals, for instance, etc.) – it can greatly change the perception, and therefore impact, of any setbacks along the way.

### Banging your drum: Communication

Major defections often happen because the partnership does not have enough information or has incorrect information, not because they have all of the information and it's bad. Opacity can quickly become poisonous when things are unsettled. This draws three points. First, leadership needs to be continually in front of the firm as the strategy is being developed and deployed, giving out constant updates – whether people ask for it or not – so that all are well informed and there is no hint of retreat, fear, or a lack of confidence from leadership. The theme here is action, not reaction. Second, silence and apathy can quickly inoculate the momentum that can come from your firm's successes and feed inertia. So, communicate and celebrate all of your successes along the way. While the degree to which a firm celebrates really depends on the appetite of the firm's culture, it can't hurt to step it up a bit, especially in the earlier stages of the deployment.

Third, if setbacks occur – and to set your expectations properly, they likely will – you need to put on your armor and hit them head-on. My 6-year-old daughter recently broke her arm very badly, requiring surgery and three days in the hospital. When she first came around the corner screaming with her arm dangling like overcooked spaghetti, my stomach dropped; I was woefully unprepared for what I saw. But, it very quickly occurred to me that I needed to calm her down and gain her cooperation until we got proper help, and to do that, she needed to believe that I was calm, that I knew what I was doing, and that I had things under control. Whether I was actually calm, informed, and in control didn't matter – I just needed her to believe it until we got some professionals involved. While this may be a bit dramatic, it is instructive. In challenging times, a partnership's strength will derive from leadership's demeanor and actions much more than just words, and a sturdy, unfazed, and proactive presence at the helm is vital.

## Fitting your leadership style to the challenge

### Recruit the right people to carry the message

Evolutionary leadership theory (ELT) is a phenomenal framework for leadership to work within. In essence, this takes an anthropological approach to the way that leadership and followership have evolved together over the course of time. An important aspect that ELT broaches is the effective "reach" of leadership, which refers to the amount of people that it directly interacts with in an efficient way, and as a result, has influence over.

Obviously, as a leader you will be the person that's quarterbacking the change initiative, and you'll be doing a lot of communicating with the firm as a whole. At the same time, there may be others within the firm that will actually be more influential than you when communicating with their respective groups. This ties into the point made earlier regarding understanding the breakdown of your firm, and might mean that your practice leaders or geographic heads are better vessels for communicating aspects of the change to their groups; it might mean that there are better ambassadors to communicate the message to particular cohorts within the firm – baby boomers, Gen X, and millennials.

While I don't have a hard and fast rule as to whom should be communicating vital information with whom – this will really depend on the inner-workings of your firm – it makes sense to take a step back and look at the composition of your firm and the various points of influence and recruit those individuals to help you carry out the message and plan.

### Communicating authentically

Being your "authentic" self is certainly a buzz term, and maybe even overused at this point. That said, the way you communicate and the quality of the communication is an incredibly important piece of the change initiative puzzle. And important to this is, above all else, that you communicate in a way that is very natural to you. There's sufficient empirical and anecdotal evidence supporting the notion that it isn't necessarily a particular way of communicating that is most influential, but more so it is *authenticity* that often carries the day.

Consider Steve Ballmer, former CEO of Microsoft, for instance. If you do a quick YouTube search on him, you'll find videos where he is just going crazy on the stage. Granted, it *is* Steve Ballmer – he walks on a different plane from most – but nevertheless, go and watch the videos and you'll see what I mean. Though he is acting in a borderline erratic way, he really pulls it off, and his employees love it.

While I don't know him personally, my strong assumption is that this highly energetic and passionate behavior is a core part of his personality. Importantly, you can see that he really cares. His intentions are believable and sincere. Now, I'm not encouraging you to behave like Steve Ballmer – unless you really are like him – but I am encouraging you to tap into your core personality strengths and leverage them to their fullest extent. Your audience will find you to be sincere, and this is what will gain buy-in from them, and your change initiative isn't going anywhere without buy-in.

No doubt you've heard of Thomas Edison's quote, "Genius is one percent inspiration, ninety nine percent perspiration." At the root of this is work – "doing." You can create the best change initiative/strategy in the world, and if now one is deploying it, it isn't going anywhere. At the same time, if you have a poorly written plan but everyone is rowing in the same direction, the chances of finding success somewhere are dramatically increased. You want people to carry out your plan. And to do so, you need them to trust that you are the person to spearhead it. This will *not* happen without sincerity, which is a direct outcome of authentic, truthful communication.

### Knowing your strengths as a leader, and delegating to bolster your weaknesses

In July of 2014 I interviewed bestselling author and journalist Adam Bryant. His *New York Times* column, *The Corner Office*, consists of leadership interviews with some of the top CEOs in the world. At that time, he had performed more than 300 interviews, and one of the common threads that he'd found among the CEOs is a brutal self-awareness: they know their strengths and weaknesses and they seek help from others. In fact, he says that this is one of the most important attributes that a leader will have as the market continues to evolve.[15]

With this in mind, be brutally honest with yourself. Where are your strengths? Where are your weaknesses? And where you are weak, be sure to shore that up with professionals in those areas. This will go a long way in building your credibility as you mobilize your change initiative/strategy. *The Failing Law Firm* uncovered a number of change efforts that failed simply because the leader was not respected enough to implement them. This might be a tough pill to swallow, but if you're looking to embark on a major change, it might be a worthwhile expenditure to have an outside party come in and assess your position within the firm to help you understand your strengths, weaknesses, and standing in the eyes of the partnership before embarking on this journey.

### *References*


1. Schultz, W., "Dopamine reward prediction error coding", March 2016. See: https://www.ncbi.nlm.nih.gov/pmc/articles/PMC4826767/
2. Martijena, I. D., and Molina, V. A., "The influence of stress on fear memory processes". March, 2012. See: *Brazilian Journal of Medical and Biological Research* http://www.scielo.br/scielo.php?script=sci_arttext&pid=S0100-879X2012000400004.
3. Samuelson, W. and Zeckhauser, R., "Status Quo Bias in Decision Making" [i] Journal of Risk and Uncertainty[/i] 1988. See: https://www.hks.harvard.edu/fs/rzeckhau/SQBDM.pdf.
4. Lyons, W., Darcy, J., Ernest, S., *Emotion*, Cambridge University Press 1985 (pg. 75).
5. Vaish, A., Grossman, T., and Woodward, A., "Not all emotions are created equal: The negativity bias in social-emotional development", May 2013. See: https://www.ncbi.nlm.nih.gov/pmc/articles/PMC3652533/.
6. Tversky, A., and Kahneman, D., *Loss Aversion in Riskless Choice: A Reference-Dependent Model*, Q J Econ, November 1991. 106 (4): 1039-1061.

7. Elliot, A. J., and Devine, P. G., "On the motivational nature of cognitive dissonance: Dissonance as psychological discomfort", *Journal of Personality and Social Psychology, Vol 67(3)*, Sep 1994, 382–394.
8. Young, S. N., "The neurobiology of human social behaviour: an important but neglected topic," *J. Psychiatry Neurosci.* 2008 Sep; 33(5): 391–392. See: https://www.ncbi.nlm.nih.gov/pmc/articles/PMC2527715/.
9. (A) Bergstrom, T. C., "Evolution of Social Behavior: Individual and Group Selection", *Journal of Economic Perspectives*, Volume 16, Number 2, 2002, Pages 67–88.
   (B) Maanen, J. V., and Schein, E. H., "Toward a Theory of Organizational Socialization", Massachusetts Institute of Technology Sloan School of Industrial Admnistration, 1978.
10. (A) Hodgkinson, G. P., "Cognitive Inertia in a Turbulent Market: the Case of UK Residential Estate Agents", *Journal of Management Studies*, Volume 34, Issue 6, November 1997, Pages 921–945.
    (B) Ferrer, C. A., Hügelschäfer, S., and Li, J., "Inertia and Decision Making", *Front Psychol.* 7: 169, 2016.
11. Parnell, D. J., *The Failing Law Firm: Symptoms and Remedies*, American Bar Association, April 2015 (Pages 79–81).
12. Parnell, D. J., *The Failing Law Firm: Symptoms and Remedies*, American Bar Association, April 2015 (Page 140, Figure 13).
13. Johnson, G., Kevan, S., and Whittington, R., *Exploring Corporate Strategy* ($8^{th}$ edition), Prentice Hall, January 2008 (Pages 365–366).
14. Parnell, D. J., "Levi Strauss & Co. CEO, Chip Bergh, *On Managing The Intersection Of Tradition And Innovation*", June 2015. See: https://www.forbes.com/sites/davidparnell/2015/06/15/levi-strauss-co-ceo-chip-bergh-on-managing-the-intersection-of-tradition-and-innovation/.
15. Parnell, D. J., "Adam Bryant of the New York Times on What Makes Great Leaders Great", July 2014. See: https://www.forbes.com/sites/davidparnell/2014/07/01/adam-bryant-of-the-new-york-times-on-great-leaders/.

# Chapter 2: Becoming change-able – Practical strategies for responding to a fast-changing world

*By Andrew Hedley, director of Hedley Consulting Ltd*

> ***"They always say time changes things, but you actually have to change them yourself."***
>
> Andy Warhol

## The importance of being change-able

I am often asked "what is the most important capability that any management team should focus on developing in its people?" My answer is always the same: it is the ability to change. Having the means to adapt to new circumstances places a firm in a position to control its environment. An inability to change means that one is beholden to the market.

We are in unchartered waters insofar as the legal profession is concerned. The past certainties of a career in the law has given way to a market in which all bets are off.

It is a challenge for all firms to understand the fast-moving world which they now inhabit and the implications for them in building a sustainable business. It is not enough, however, to understand the forces in play and where they are leading but also to chart a course through such turbulent seas.

Most importantly, firms need to be change-able to capitalize on new opportunities and mitigate emergent threats.

Being change-able means developing a suite of skills which, when deployed in union, allow the firm to approach the challenges which it faces with high-levels of confidence in a successful outcome. Here we discuss the application of best-practices in change management to the legal sector whilst also reflecting on some of the peculiarities found within law firms and how these might be factored into any change initiative, so maximizing the chances of success.

## The key components of a successful change programme

Not surprisingly, change has been an area of extensive academic study over the past 20 years. John Kotter is widely acknowledged as the world's leading thinker on the subject. In his best-selling book *Leading Change*, Kotter argues that successful change is an issue of leadership rather than management.

Management techniques are important, of course, in dealing with the complexities which will be inevitable is charting and implementing change. However, it is through leadership that success is most effectively delivered. It is incumbent on the firm's leaders to build commitment to change if any process is to maximize its potential of a successful outcome.

Kotter's work highlights eight stages of an effective major change programme which forms a template against which any project can be planned:

- Stage one: Establishing a sense of urgency
- Stage two: Creating a guiding coalition
- Stage three: Developing the vision and strategy
- Stage four: Communicating the change vision
- Stage five: Empowering broad-based action
- Stage six: Generating short-term wins
- Stage seven: Consolidating gains and producing more change
- Stage eight: Anchoring new approaches in the culture

Change, both great and small, can be delivered by systematically applying this process. Each stage, however, needs to be viewed through the lens of the legal profession and the culture of any particular firm.

The most common problem encountered in my work is an almost irresistible desire to short-circuit the process and jump straight to stage four (both within the partner group and then the firm as a whole). In such a short-circuited scenario, the managing partner and a small team goes into a room, locks the door behind it and crafts a strategy.

When they emerge, this group will be acutely aware of the need for change, have high urgency, and be united in their beliefs. The vision for the future and strategy which they develop may have merit but it will almost certainly fail completely or, at best, deliver sub-optimal results. This is because their palpable urgency is not shared and the vision that they have created is not embedded widely enough across the key stakeholders in the business.

Unsurprisingly, there is nearly always deep-seated resistance at two levels. First, those not involved in the vision and strategy making don't necessarily understand why change is needed. Second, even if they can be retrospectively convinced, they have been emasculated by the process, have no emotional commitment to it and will likely resist the imposition of any vision no matter how compelling or logical. The first three stages of Kotter's process ensure that this happens with the subsequent components ensuring that this vision is effectively and enduringly delivered.

### Stage one: Establishing a sense of urgency

The first task is to establish a sense of urgency across the whole firm, which poses considerable challenges for partnerships riddled with complacency. Why do we need to change? What will be the consequences of not changing? When will those consequences impact on the firm? These are the three questions which need to be addressed.

Change is difficult at both a personal and organizational level. In many firms, the autonomy afforded by a profession has allowed partners to build a very personal approach to their working life – effectively creating a cocoon in which they are able to function within the overall framework of their firm but with substantial personal discretion and latitude in terms of behaviors and working practices. They have created a work environment within which they are very comfortable. Psychology tells us that people will only really consider and undertake significant change when they believe that the pain of change will be less than the pain of staying where they are.

In simple terms people need to be clear to why change is not only desirable but necessary for the longer-term viability of the firm. By raising the sense of urgency and creating the burning platform in a considered way, not seeking to create panic but rather to argue for a structured and systematic change process, the leadership team is able to create the environment that is critical to the overall programme.

### Stage two: Creating a guiding coalition

It is then important to ensure that those involved in arriving at a vision of what the future needs to look like are representative of the power and influence structure of the firm. The purpose of the guiding coalition is both to consult widely and to engage fully those most able to contribute to the change process.

In this sense, whilst such a group will certainly have significant representation from those with management responsibility within the firm it should also include the key opinion formers and thinkers, regardless of whether or not they have a formal management role.

**Stage three: Developing the vision and strategy**

The creation of vision and strategy is a huge subject area, beyond the scope of this article, but experience suggests that successful visions and strategies share a small number of common traits within the law firm market.

Firstly, they are clear and easy to understand. This is critical given the nature of law firms and the fact that strategy can only be given true effect through the actions of people. If people do not understand what the firm is trying to achieve, and what their role is on this journey, then the most intellectually robust strategy will fail. In simple terms, each person in the firm should be clear about what they need to do differently in order to play their part in realising the vision.

Next, the good strategy must be actionable within the firm's resources (either those it already has or those which can be acquired). It must be very stretching but ultimately achievable. It must be rooted in the reality of the firm's competitive position and market opportunities rather than a flight of fantasy, playing more to the egos of the partners than an objective analysis of the opportunity. Actionability also encompasses culture – answering the question of what sort of firm we want to be from a cultural perspective.

Finally, good strategy is measurable. It allows us to understand where we are now, where we are aiming to be and what progress we have made.

**Stage four: Communicating the change vision**

A structured (and ongoing) communication process is vital. Any change initiative has the potential to affect morale and performance. Indeed, research shows that this is often the case as people come to terms with a new reality. These concerns and tensions are reduced when information, support, guidance, and opportunities to feed back at critical stages in the change implementation process are factored in.

At the outset of the communications programme, the aim should be to raise awareness of what is proposed and why it is necessary. A common human reaction may be denial or frustration; the focus of the leadership team must be on building commitment. Such emotions will often be shared openly and can be dealt with quickly and effectively.

However, as the change process moves on, it will be vital for the firm to increase levels of understanding among its people about how the change will happen, how it will improve working practices, and the benefits that it will bring. During this part of the change cycle, hidden feelings of anger, confusion, and resentment may emerge. It is therefore crucial that transitional support is offered throughout this phase.

### Stage five: Empowering broad-based action

Major change can only be given effect by empowering people across the firm. The small leadership team cannot achieve organizational change by itself; it is only by creating a platform for broadly based action that change can be hard-wired into the business at both an emotional and pragmatic level.

A focus on clarifying roles and responsibilities, is key. This is the point at which investment should be made in equipping people with the new skills they will need to succeed in future.

By providing support, the firm will be able to achieve high levels of engagement and commitment from its people to the change process. If done well, a shift in mindset can be achieved.

### Stage six: Generating short-term wins

Momentum is critical for any change programme and it is important to ensure that evidence of success is delivered at any early stage. People need to see progress, to build belief and to overcome the natural fears and concerns that run the risk of jeopardising the initiative.

For this reason, the smart leadership team focuses on creating some short-term wins. By getting runs on the board, fear is allayed, progress is demonstrated and those who may still have doubts about the ability of the firm to deliver have these assuaged.

Those at the vanguard of change will become advocates themselves. They will have seen the positive effects of working differently and want to help others to benefit too. They will be actively involved in the change effort.

### Stage seven: Consolidating gains and producing more change

Once built momentum needs to be maintained. It is not enough simply to overcome the first hurdle or provide evidence of the first success.

These initial wins must be used as catalysts to accelerate more change and build an impetus which becomes unstoppable. A danger for any team is to rest on its laurels after early success, believing that the job is done and so allowing deep-seated and hard-to-budge beliefs to take hold once again.

### Stage eight: Anchoring new approaches in the culture

Change has been given effect when the new approach is simply regarded as "the way we do things around here". More importantly the emotional and philosophical shift of mindset means that the firm is then in an excellent position to make continuous change simply part of how it does business more widely.

Having been through a successful change programme, confidence is high and the path is clear to engage in an ongoing change cycle. This is hugely important in a legal sector which is moving at pace in unpredictable ways.

Firms which are change-able have the ability to seize control of their future direction and success. Those unable to foster a change orientation are at the mercy of the market, the client, and the competition.

## Dealing with rogue elephants and the strategically non-compliant

In working with law firms over the last two decades, I have observed many ways in which change is resisted, whether overtly or covertly, consciously or sub-consciously. I broadly categorize those who resist change into two types – the rogue elephants and the strategically non-compliant.

The rogue elephant change resistor is easy to identify. They are few in number but they are very large, bombastic, and make their views known to anyone who will listen. They trample around the metaphorical jungle and have the ability to cause lots of damage, delay, distraction, and panic.

However, because they are easy to identify the leadership team that is serious about change can develop strategies to deal with the rogue elephants – figuratively speaking, these range from building a stockade around them, perhaps taking them to a different reservation, all the way through to the purchase of a 12-bore shotgun!

In the case of the rogue elephants, we know who they are and the question is how we address the challenge that they pose. This is a leadership issue boiled down to its essence.

The second group can be much more demanding to deal with. These are the people who sit in meetings and nod, who attend presentations and never have a question. These are the people who then return to their desks, put their heads down and carry on as they always have.

They are not disruptive, they do not challenge management but rather they do nothing, quite literally. By doing nothing they mire the change programme.

I term them the strategically non-compliant because they make an active choice not to engage but rather live in the hope that "the next big idea" will eventually blow over. Their memories are long and they doubtless recall the last big idea which was never realised, finding comfort in the fact that they were right not to waste their time and instead stick to what they had always done.

Of course, by not engaging they are significant contributors to the failure of change initiatives.

Dealing with the strategically non-compliant is a challenge for many firms, something which we discuss further in the next section. Again leadership is needed but of a longer-term, more granular nature to unlock and realise the wider potential of the firm.

## Adopting Pareto for change

Readers will no doubt be familiar with the Pareto effect or 80:20 rule (named after the Italian economist Vilfredo Pareto) which states that, for many events, roughly 80 percent of the effects come from 20 percent of the causes.

A number of years ago, I observed how many firms involved in a change process focused first on getting those most resistant to change to "get on board" with the programme. It also struck me that a large percentage of the firm were held back by the delays that were experienced in such an approach.

My suggestion, and one which has proved successful in numerous subsequent projects, was to focus efforts on those who want to change (provided always that recalcitrant few are not being overly disruptive to the process). In the first change cycle focus on taking 80 percent of the firm with you.

The second change cycle can then focus on converting 80 percent of the 20 percent who remain. Some of these will fall into one or more of the following categories – those who thought the firm was not serious, those who have experienced failed change programmes in the past and were not prepared to invest in a potentially futile exercise and those who are psychologically unable to accept that change is needed. By bringing 80 percent of the 20 percent on board over the second change cycle, only 4 percent hard-line change resistors remain.

The third change cycle then focuses on converting 80 percent of the 4 percent. After these three cycles, less than 1 percent of the original population will remain. At this point the firm has an overwhelming mandate to demand that those still out-standing to come on board or consider whether the new firm is somewhere that is suitable for them.

## Communication is at the core of a successful programme

A structured, comprehensive, and ongoing communication process is vital if the chances of success are to be maximized. This is central to the role of the law firm leader.

Any change initiative has the potential to affect morale and performance. Indeed, research shows that this is often the case as people come to terms with a new reality. These concerns and tensions are reduced when information, support, guidance, and opportunities to feed back at critical stages in the change implementation process are factored in.

At the outset of the change programme, the aim should be to raise awareness of what is proposed and why it is necessary. A common human reaction may be denial or frustration; the focus of the leadership team must be on building commitment. Such emotions will often be shared openly and can be dealt with quickly and effectively.

However, as the change process moves on, it will be vital for the firm to increase levels of understanding among its people about how the change will happen, how it will improve working practices and the benefits that it will bring. During this part of the change cycle, hidden feelings of anger, confusion, and resentment may emerge. It is therefore crucial that transitional support is offered throughout this phase.

Clear communication, focused on clarifying roles and responsibilities, is key. This is also the point at which investment should be made in equipping people with the new skills they will need to succeed in future. By providing support, the firm will be able to achieve high levels of engagement and commitment from its people to the change process. If done well, a shift in mindset can be achieved. Those at the vanguard of change will become advocates themselves. They will have seen the positive effects of working differently and want to help others to benefit too. They will be actively involved in the change effort.

Creating and maintaining momentum is important. Demonstrating that the climb will be worth the view is critical to bring about the sorts of behavioral changes that are required and to maximize the chances of success for any programme. Once the initial eagerness has waned, law firm leaders should frequently communicate, using a range if channels, further incremental evidence of progress in order to refuel ambition and maintain momentum.

## Winning hearts and minds to create a change-able firm

A firm that is change-able doesn't just have a good understanding of change management techniques, reinforced with a robust set of tried and tested processes. It also has the ability to engage its people in a journey, to move from a current state to a desired one. It is this engagement of people which can be most challenging. Without it, any change process will most likely flounder.

For most, intellectual buy-in for a new initiative is not the fundamental obstacle which needs to be overcome. Winning minds is the easy part of the equation; it is winning hearts which represents the more formidable challenge. Progress here rests on the firm's ability to build and maintain emotional commitment so creating a longer-term shift of attitude, approach, and delivery. That is the real measure of success.

It is often said that there are three types of firm – those which make things happen, those which watch things happen, and those which wonder what happened! Use change management strategies, tools, and tactics to ensure that you are in the first not the last category.

# Chapter 3:
# A framework for effective change management

*By Neryl East, writer, academic, speaker, and communication specialist*

Setting aside the dismal failure rate of many change management programmes, what can be learned from those that do succeed? While there is no one size-fits-all-approach and every organization has its own idiosyncrasies, successful change programmes have some traits in common, including the balance between process and people.

The last decade has seen a shift away from the more radical, back-to-the-drawing board approach to change advocated through systems like BPR. While top-down transformation and business reinvention held a certain appeal for business leaders in the 1990s, the outrage provoked by mass downsizing led to a reduction in such heavy-hitting strategies. Management Today[1] writes that: "BPR may retain some of its logic today, but sensible bosses proceed with extreme caution."

Other approaches, such as appreciative inquiry, focus heavily on involving stakeholders in positive discussion about change and opening the organization up to new possibilities. Positive focus is the first step and ideas; and processes follow.

There are many change management frameworks, strategies, and approaches; and not every model adapts to every organizational situation. Some presented here are well known while others arise from specific cases. Many others are described in change management literature.

### McKinsey 7-S model

Developed in the late seventies, the 7-S model sets out interrelated factors that influence an organization's ability to change and focuses on coordination rather than structure, in improving organizational effectiveness. The model consists of seven factors:

- **Strategy** – The integrated vision and direction of the company as well as the manner in which it communicates and implements that vision and direction;

- **Structure** – The form of the organizational chart and interconnections between positions in the organizational hierarchy;
- **Systems** – The procedures and routine processes required to perform the work, including the ways information moves through the organization;
- **Staff** – The personnel categories within the organization, for example, marketeers, engineers.
- **Style** – The characterization of the ways key managers set priorities and behave in order to achieve the organization's goals;
- **Skills** – The distinctive capabilities of the organization as a whole; and
- **Shared values** – The core beliefs underlying the organization's existence and its expectations of its members. Values act as in organization's conscience and provide guidance in times of crisis.

The framework's lack of hierarchy suggests that it is difficult to make significant progress in one part of the organization in isolation. All steps need equal consideration.

### Kotter's eight-step process

Dr John Kotter[2] developed his process after 30 years of research into why so many change initiatives fail. He encourages organizations to follow these eight steps and improve their ability to change:

- Acting with urgency – Kotter says a sense of urgency is needed to get the cooperation required to drive a significant change effort. Most companies ignore this step, with many underestimating how hard it is to move people from their comfort zones;
- Developing the guiding coalition – Based on no one individual being able to singly develop and communicate the right vision, eliminate the obstacles and lead and anchor the change projects. Gathering the right coalition of people to lead a change initiative is critical to success;
- Developing a change vision – To simplify the many detailed decisions to follow, motivate people to act in the right direction and coordinate actions;
- Communicating the vision for buy-in – Using every effective communication channel possible to broadcast the vision;

- Empowering broad-based action – Removing as many barriers as possible and unleashing people to do their best work;
- Generating short-term wins – The guiding coalition is critical in identifying significant, visible improvements than can happen between six and 18 months;
- Don't let up – Drive new behaviors and practices into the culture, do not become complacent if there are early successes; and
- Make change stick – In Kotter's process, cultural change comes last, not first and he urges organizations to be able to prove that the new way is superior to the old.

### A cross-cultural framework

Implementation of a knowledge management framework within a section of the Abu Dhabi government[3] found success through steps that focused heavily on getting buy-in from stakeholders and generating culturally appropriate communication:

- Leadership alignment – Recognizing that a transformation programme is more likely to succeed if the entire leadership team is fully aware and supportive of the process. In this case, a well-attended leadership workshop included an artist drawing key points and phrases during the discussion, to allow participants to process the messages using visuals.
- Knowledge management teams – Setting up on-the-ground teams in each part of the business participating in the change programme. In this example four teams were established, augmented by more than 1,000 knowledge champions across the organization who were equipped to become super-users of the new system. The champions were kept engaged through weekly meetings, group exercises, external speakers, and an award programme.
- Communication – Delivering a phased communication programme including strong and relevant branding of the programme, a collaborative intranet site, letters and e-newsletters, information sessions, promotional material, external media coverage, and a promotional film. Cultural issues played a part in this case; for example, in a culture where there is reluctance to admit mistakes, running "lessons learned" sessions to discuss what went wrong was not an effective approach.

- Training and knowledge transfer – Allowing users of the new system to learn through observation and participation and ensuring "champions" are also trained in soft skills.

Key factors in the project's overall success included:

- A clear understanding of cultural aspects in the design of communication material;
- Using different types of communication over a long period;
- Recruiting champions as change agents and advocates;
- Involving staff as much as possible at every stage of the project;
- Bringing the change to life through day-to-day scenarios that people could relate to;
- Giving feedback and communicating progress; and
- Using best-practice models but tailoring to meet the needs of the organization and its culture.

### Framework for behavioral change

Lawson and Price[4] argue that, despite the large number of available organizational improvement programmes, successful change still depends on persuading large numbers of people to alter the way they work and that CEOs, in effect, must shift the mind-sets of their staff. They put forward four conditions for changing attitudes at work:

1. Having a purpose to believe in – People must believe in the organization's overall purpose and understand the part they have to play in the "unfolding drama of the company's fortunes".
2. Having reinforcement systems – When a company's goals for new behavior are not positively reinforced, employees are less likely to adopt such behavior consistently.
3. Having consistent role models – Recognizing that in any organization, people model their behavior on those they see in positions of influence. Role modelling by individuals must be confirmed by the various groups with which people identify. "Change must be meaningful to key groups at each level of the organization." A leader could be brilliant at communicating and role modelling a change, but that good work is easily undone if middle managers or work

groups are griping about the change and sneering that "we've heard all this before, it will never work".

4. Putting the approach into practice – Recognizing that any change programme comes with "much disruption and risk", but basing it on proven principles will maximise the likelihood of success.

### A change-readiness assessment

Before selecting a framework or embarking on any change activities, many writers on change management encourage taking a long, hard look at the organization to determine whether it is in fact ready for the change that is planned. Is the pain of change likely to produce the desired results, or is the status quo – or a smaller change – a better option for now? A change-readiness assessment can include gauging how much employees know about the external environment of the firm, as well as gathering intelligence on the internal culture and structural issues.

*HRMagazine*[5] suggests a simple process to evaluate an organization's capacity to take on additional planned change:

- Develop a list of the major change activities currently taking place and identify which ones compete for budget, staff time, and other resources;
- Estimate the level of effort required for each activity; and
- Compare this required effort to the change initiative being considered.

It says assessment can also be carried out by observing employee behavior to gauge possible reactions to change; auditing how the company communicates the "why, when, and how" of change initiatives; documenting employee reactions to the change process through interviews and group discussions; and using structured survey methods to determine the organization's change readiness.

Kehoe[6] recommends rating the organization on a scale from one to five across 12 areas:

- Level of staff commitment to the proposed changes;
- Degree to which staff were engaged in previous change initiatives;
- Agreed level of follow-up to be provided after implementation;
- Agreed level of support to be provided during implementation;

- Management competence to manage staff performance during implementation;
- Evidence available to verify the proposed change will be for the better;
- Degree to which staff are likely to value the changes;
- Staff clarity about what they will be asked to do differently;
- Staff belief in the proposed changes;
- Alignment of staff perceptions about what is important when implementing the changes;
- Degree to which staff are prepared to share knowledge and skills during implementation; and
- Degree to which staff are likely to willingly carry out the new behaviors.

He describes a rating of 49 or above as: "You're as ready as you'll ever be. Good luck." While 24 or below is more like: "Start now and the change process will be a constant uphill battle."

Others recommend taking a further step back and analysing the issue at the core of the proposed change itself. Sharon Drew Morgen's *Facilitative Questions for Change and Innovative Decision-making*[7] take the participant through a checklist of thought provoking queries such as:

- What would you need to see/hear/feel to recognize when it was time to do something different?
- How do you plan on bringing (interested parties) into the decisions you need to make?
- How will you manage the situation if they believe they will be harmed by the change?
- What will success look like?
- How can you be sure that the problem will remain solved over time?

### Taking the plunge

Assuming the organization is deemed to be ready for the change, when should the implementation begin? The timing of a change programme is usually determined by the nature of the change itself, for example, whether it is being implemented in anticipation of an external event or factor, in response to a change in business trends or as a reaction to a more pressing issue or crisis.

It stands to reason that the more proactive and strategic the change, the better the chance of being well-prepared and moving ahead with confidence in the organization's state of change readiness. A change introduced abruptly in a crisis situation will test the mettle of the organization's leadership, communication abilities; and systems and processes. Poorly managed change in a change-resistant organization is likely to cause people to "dig in their heels" and sabotage the change, either openly or covertly.

*HRMagazine*[8] highlights five types of "enabling structures" which are likely to help a change initiative get traction. These are:

- Pilot programmes;
- Training programmes;
- Employee retention programmes;
- Outplacement programmes; and
- Reward systems.

For example, pilot programmes allow a change to be implemented on a small scale and for feedback to be gathered from managers and staff. Rewards can be introduced at different stages of the change to motivate involvement.

Bernadez[9] recommends a highly tactical approach with the first phase likened to guerrilla warfare where small, low-risk changes are introduced and slowly develop into bigger, organization-wide changes. Once the programme has some traction, the "waterfall effect" comes into play: "Each time the measured results of a successful, low-budget micro-experience of real performance improvement reach senior management, a waterfall of contagious interest is put into motion, empowering further projects."

Finally, the "afterburner follow-up" employs the principle of a plane taking off on the short runway of an aircraft carrier and re-using combustion gases to increase momentum. Successes need to be publicised and successful models exchanged. Friendly competition is stimulated within the organization, change champions are used in an ongoing role to train and mentor staff; and track records are highly visible throughout the company.

Shorter-term improvements can be the linchpin of a change initiative.[10] Even if employees seem to embrace an overall change programme, they must be convinced that a new vision and direction can make a difference to them and the organization in the long term. Short-term achievements are proof that the change efforts are worth all the downsides. Those smaller wins help overcome the fear, uncertainty, and resistance that frequently go hand in hand with change.

While resistance to change is discussed at various points throughout this report, it is worthy of a special mention in the overall picture. According to Kotter:[11] "You must recognize that the forces in organizations that maintain the status quo are powerful and everywhere." As another writer expresses it, facing resistance "may well be the greatest challenge for all change agents".[12] An online forum writer suggests that, in fact, "people don't resist change, people resist being changed" while another equates resistance with a lack of individual readiness for change, which can be addressed through careful, one-on-one attention to the aspects causing them stress.

One way to work with naysayers is to let them experience the problems first-hand. The example is cited of a New York City police commissioner who wanted his workers to fully understand crime problems on the city's subway system. After being required to ride the subways for a month and witness the extent of petty crime and the reaction of nervous passengers, they were enthusiastic about taking action to correct the problem. Within six months, the system was safer and crime rates were down.

Drotos[13] points out that a corporate restructure or downsizing initiative can have remarkable similarities to a battle:

- "Unnerving sights and sounds (the tears of the recently laid off, the sight of a recently abandoned desk or workstation);
- Casualties (what do you say or do after someone has been outsourced?);
- Confusion;
- Lack of information;
- Feelings of isolation;
- Communication breakdowns;
- Physical discomfort and fatigue;
- Stress and mental fatigue; and
- The need for continuous operations in the face of all this."

It becomes critical to provide support to remaining staff. Survivors may not be able to move beyond the battle scene until they can process their feelings about the change and any losses that have accompanied it.

## Appreciative inquiry

At the other end of the spectrum from the battlefield analogy is the field of appreciative inquiry, a rapidly growing "approach to organizational change that emphasizes and builds on a company's strengths and potential".[14] In its simplest terms, appreciative inquiry is about focusing on positive elements to gain positive results. As McKenna[15] points out: "When you focus your attention on what's not working, all you'll see is what's not working."

Appreciative inquiry begins with a deep analysis of what works well in the organization. It aims to involve as many stakeholders as possible; for example, if a proposed change was about to impact on a hospital, the approach would involve patients as well as staff. Rather than looking for problems and identifying potential solutions to change the company culture, it asks participants to focus on what they want to see. Appreciative inquiry practitioner Dr Diana Whitney[16] says: "We don't expect every organization to be at its best, but we do know in every organization we have our moments when we're at the top of our game. [Appreciative Inquiry] begins by studying those times."

An example of this in action might be found in an organization concerned about high staff turnover rates. What might traditionally have been a negative discussion about the number of employees leaving and the reasons why would transform into a conversation about staff retention and creating a workplace that attracts and holds people through a sense of loyalty. That change in thinking gives rise to positive strategies. While Whitney concedes there are some issues that must be tackled head on: "In most cases, 98 percent of the time, reframing the negative into the affirmative moves the organization and gives it positive possibilities".

## Leading the change

Assuming readiness, framework and timing are clear, who is best to lead a change management initiative? The Change Management Institute's survey of change managers[18] found that respondents gave the highest rating to internal teams – those seconded or otherwise 100 percent applied to the change programme – as the most suitable leaders of change management. That was followed by department heads, the board and external/independent change management professionals. External "name brand" global consultancy firms fared the worst in suitability ratings. "It is rarely effective to add change management to an already overloaded internal team, who might not have the capacity or capability to deliver, without significant assistance," the survey report noted.

Wherever they come from in the organization, change leaders must be adept at instilling a firm and optimistic picture of the future, while managing their own response to the change. This requires a level of self-awareness and an understanding of their reactions. Kotter[19] points out middle managers are increasingly being drawn into the change leadership role because organizations can have two or three major change efforts underway simultaneously. Leading change, which was once only the domain of a charismatic figurehead, "has increasingly become central to middle managers and their career success" and they are not just "passive followers of some great leader".

Trahant, Warner Burke, and Koonce[20] emphasize the need for the organization's leadership to first change its thinking before any broader change can be successfully implemented. They describe the process as "leadershift", because it requires business leaders to think about change in new, multidimensional ways that might not have occurred to them before. Their principles of leadershift include:

- Understand the external environment;
- Enlist people's passion and energy to support the company mission;
- Change people's behavior, not just their beliefs, values, and work schedules;
- Let service to customers drive the company structure;
- Give people the systems to support them in their work;
- Remember that employees are people, too;
- Give employees what they need to succeed; and
- Teamwork is critical.

Clearly, the stakes of change are high, the risks significant and the choice of approaches potentially overwhelming.

**Key tools**

- There is no one-size-fits-all model for organizational change. Choose an approach that best fits the organization;
- A change-readiness assessment can be a useful exercise for your organization; and
- There is an emerging trend towards approaches such as appreciative inquiry, which focuses on building on an organization's strengths and involving all stakeholders.

*A version of this chapter was first published in East, N.,* Implementing an Effective Change Management Strategy, *London, ARK Group, 2011.*

### *References*

1. "Brainfood: Master class 1. – Re-engineering", *Management Today*, June 2005.
2. The John Kotter website, www.kotterinternational.com.
3. Murphy, E., "Change Management Successes and Lessons Learned in Creating a Knowledge Sharing Culture across the Department for Municipal Affairs, Abu Dhabi". See: www.acmp.info/conference/files/Murphy-2010.pdf, 2010.
4. Lawson, E. and Price, C., "The psychology of change management", *McKinsey Quarterly*, June 2003. See: www.mckinseyquarterly.com/Organization/Change_Management.
5. "Change management: the HR strategic imperative as a business partner", *HR Magazine*, December 2007.
6. Kehoe, D., *Leading and Managing Change*, McGraw Hill, Australia, 2007.
7. For further information visit: www.businessballs.com/innovationdecision-makingfacilitation.htm.
8. "Change management: the HR strategic imperative as a business partner", *HR Magazine*, December 2007.
9. Bernadez, M., "Start SMALL, change BIG", *Management Review*, June 1997.
10. "Short-Term Wins – The Linchpin of a Change Initiative", *Managing Change to Reduce Resistance*, Harvard Business School Press, 2005.
11. "How to Get Aboard a Major Change Effort; An interview with John Kotter", *Managing Change to Reduce Resistance*, Harvard Business School Press, 2005.
12. *Ibid.*
13. Chip Drotos, J., "When organizations downsize", *Behavioral Health Management*, July-August 2003.
14. Krattenmaker, T., "Change through Appreciative Inquiry", *Managing Change to Reduce Resistance*, Harvard Business School Press, 2005.

15. McKenna, P., "Leading Change: Adaptive Approaches To Implementing Your Best Intentions", www.patrickmckenna.com, 2010.
16. President of Corporation for Positive Change, Diana Whitney, and Associate Professor of Graduate Management at LTU, Jackie Stavros, describe the change method of appreciative inquiry for identifying a company's positive core to heighten energy and vision for positive change and growth. See: www.blogtalkradio.com/waynehurlbert/2008/08/22/jackie-stavrosdiana-whitney-appreciative-inquiry-handbookfor-leaders-of-change 2008.
17. *Ibid.*
18. "Challenge of Change Australia", survey conducted by Executives Online and the Change Management Institute, www.changemanagement-institute.com, September 2009.
19. "How to Get Aboard a Major Change Effort; An interview with John Kotter", *Managing Change to Reduce Resistance*, Harvard Business School Press, 2005.
20. Trahant, B, Warner Burke, W. and Koonce, R., "12 Principles of Organizational Transformation", *Management Review*, September 1997.

Chapter 4:

# Once an opportunity is identified, what next? Creating and driving an innovation agenda

*By Duncan Hart, director of Duncan Hart Consulting*

***"We take a seed capital approach to all the services we start offering, take it to market, then readjust it. It is a low-risk model of innovation for law firms"***

Wim Dejonghe, Global Managing Partner, Allen & Overy

Once an opportunity is identified, it then becomes a question of resourcing the initiative and crafting a solution based on insights that are gained as that initiative is progressed. Obviously, there will be plenty of "failures" in this approach, but the importance of growing a tolerance for failure cannot be over emphasised. It is not so much that failure should be "celebrated"; it is simply that it is from such failures that the firm can learn what might succeed next time. That failure provides the opportunity to learn and failure itself is a significant indicator of the amount of innovative experimentation being carried out within the firm. Again, the central thesis is that, whatever the apparent merits of the initial analysis, and no matter how promising the opportunity appears to be, there is no substitute for testing the new service in the market as soon as possible and detecting any fundamental flaws in that analysis and the service's underlying assumptions. The range of possible outcomes from such an approach should be as wide as the ambition, risk tolerance, and the resources of the firm permit.

## A "stage-gate" approach

Once an opportunity has been identified in the "analysis" process, how should that opportunity now be progressed to the mutual satisfaction of the firm and its innovators? I outline in detail below a multi-stage or gate process with a careful evaluation at each stage, though clearly there will be many more informal meetings between "gates". While informal assistance and frequent contact is desirable to keep any project moving, I strongly urge the retention of something akin to the more "formal" requirements set out in this chapter. A rigorous approach to such projects underlines to all concerned that the firm is serious about its innovation strategy. What's more, the need to keep all stakeholders (particularly "corporate anti-bodies" at bay) and acquainted with the project's progress is essential. In addition, the innovation committee will find it very difficult to monitor and assist groups if their internal processes (and the rigor behind them) are not followed, particularly when any project gets to the testing of its "minimum viable product" in the market and exposing it to clients. The failure of most innovations can usually be very clearly linked to a lack of disciplined testing at that stage and the committee should be very clear about this while at the same time making support and resources available to give the innovation every chance of success.

Figure 1 outlines the key stages and the activities that should take place between gates, both on the project team's part and by the innovation committee. The stage-gate process is not only designed to enable the appropriate project management disciplines to be applied, but as importantly, it incorporates key learnings and particularly processes adopted from the "start-up" environment.

### Innovation action – Lessons from the "start-up" environment and the stage-gate process

As in any entrepreneurial environment, the gap between the idea and its successful commercialisation is immense. Even more so in the field of professional services where lawyers are happy to advise others what to do but seldom bear the full commercial consequences for the failure of that advice. Most lawyers did not become lawyers to undertake risky commercial ventures; after all, "law" is a "safe" profession, rather than a hotbed of entrepreneurial activity.

The stage-gate process outlined above owes much to the experience of those that have led much of the discussion and debate around today's "start-up" culture and evidence gleaned from those who have brought invention and innovation from "whiteboard" to market in a "commercialization" process. In particular, the concepts of "lean innovation" developed by Eric Ries[1] are of particular relevance in encouraging a "fail fast", "learning" approach to developing the skills so lacking in the professional services sector.

The key learnings that I draw upon cover several stages common to many successful "start-ups" and require:

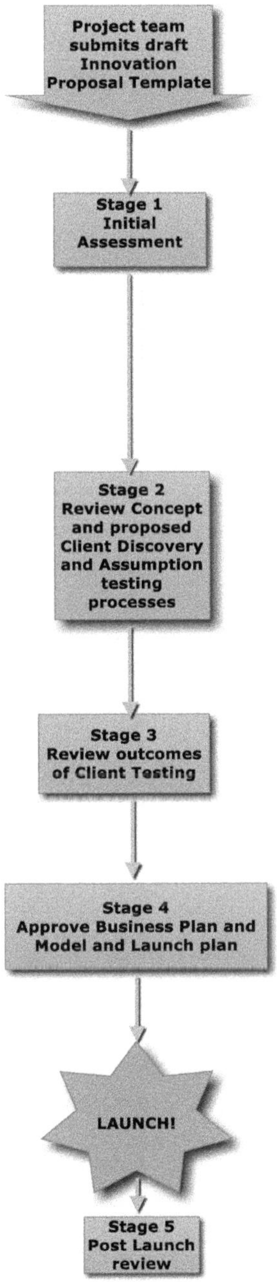


*Figure 1: Innovation project stage-gate process – Key stages and activities*

- Evaluation – What are the key assumptions upon which the idea is based?
- Resource allocation and early support;
- Rapid prototyping – The creation of a "minimum viable product" (MVP);
- Testing key assumptions – Learning "outside the office";[2]
- Evaluating and responding to client reaction – Data, detail, and response;
- "Pivot" or "kill" decisions; and
- Scaling for success.

If the firm is not prepared to embrace this all-important implementation phase with as much if not more commitment than the familiar "whiteboard" analysis process, then there is no realistic chance of success and opportunities to learn will be minimized. It is likely that the exercise will simply degenerate into the all-too-familiar hiatus that we have all seen after a typical "firm retreat": a mass of barely-thought-out ideas, projects, and suggestions with absolutely no idea as to how, if ever, the firm means to sensibly evaluate which should proceed, let alone how it might be brought to market, or how anything could be learnt from the experience of trying to do so.

The "stage-gate" process is designed to ensure that a similar approach is adopted. The "gates" cannot be passed until the pre-requisite steps have been undertaken and the appropriate groundwork laid to give the initiative concerned the greatest chance of success. It also ensures that all such projects are subject to the same rigour and teams are given clear guidance as to what is expected at each stage of the process. Equally, it ensures both the leadership team and most importantly the innovation committee provide appropriate resources to get the team through the whole process, or at least be clear about why and where the project failed to meet expectations.

An Innovation Proposal Template (see Figure 3) is also suggested as a means of encouraging the project team to address a number of these key issues before submitting its proposal to the innovation committee.

### The role of the leadership team in the stage-gate process

In the creation and implementation of any innovation project, the leadership team must maintain a high level of credibility through careful and obvious support for its programme, even though much of the day-to-day work will be carried out by its innovation committee. Processes must be put in place and clearly supported to deal with a range of issues which often fatally compromise projects of this nature.

Requirements of the firm and its innovation team in these circumstances can be grouped under three broad headings: leadership, resources, and people. These requirements include:

1. *Leadership*

a. Top management is committed to the "innovation project" as a whole;

b. Strong leadership is provided to support project teams through the creation of an innovation committee;

c. Sufficient time and resources are allocated through the innovation committee to properly fund and resource project teams;

d. Sufficient time and resources are made available to the innovation committee to ensure it can encourage and initiate innovation projects and carry out its review function;

e. There is a clear appetite for risk and it is encouraged;

f. The issue of how participants in such projects are to be recognized, and particularly how participants can be protected from criticism for devoting time and resources to such projects, is sufficiently considered. In particular, specific protocols need to be developed which recognise that participants' remuneration, adherence to budgetary requirements, and other expectations of participants are balanced fairly;

g. Recognition is provided in the sense of being incorporated with any appraisal processes utilised within the firm;

h. The leadership team, and specifically the innovation committee, remain actively involved and are seen to promote innovation projects;

i. Any decision-making process with respect to the innovation agenda is transparent and shared widely; and

j. The leadership creates and regularly reviews its range of key criteria for projects to qualify for support and development – e.g., costs, delivery time, return on investment.

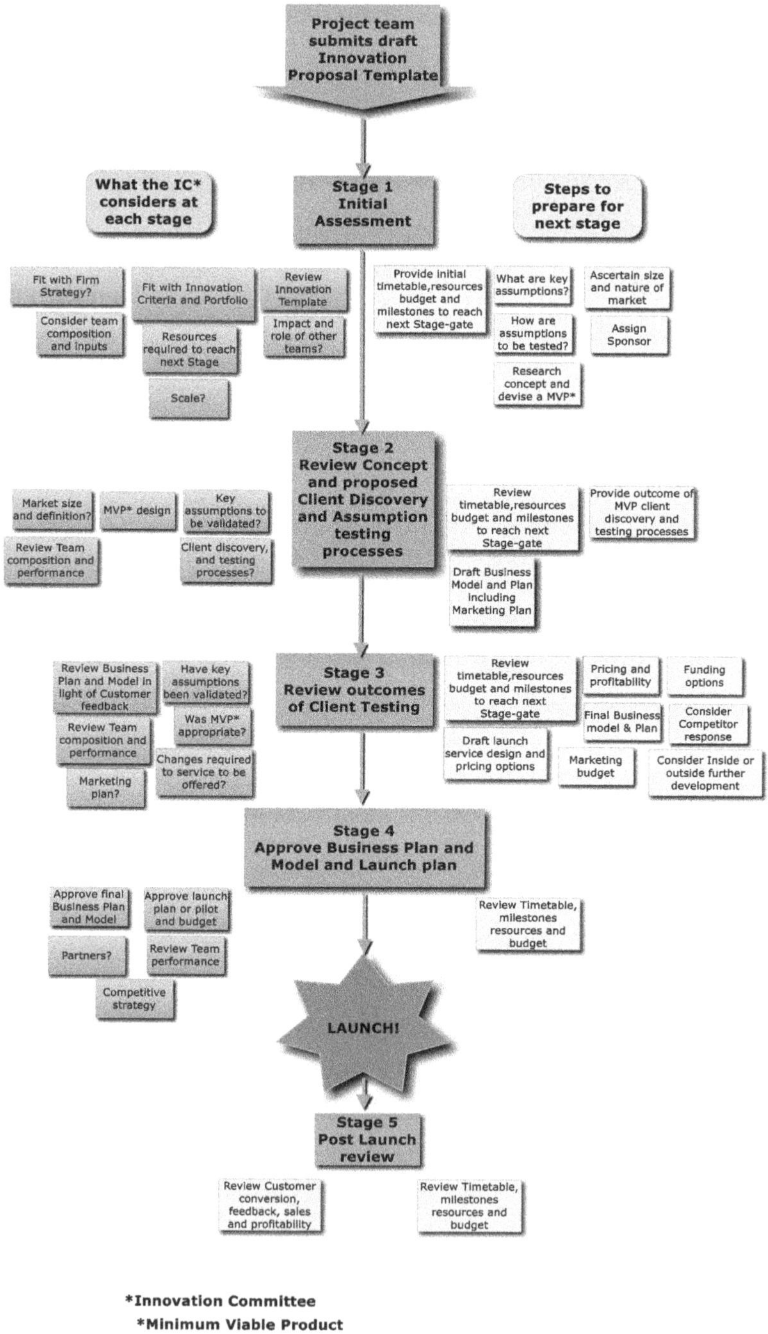


*Figure 2: Innovation project stage-gate process in detail*

*2. Resources*

a. Appropriate resources and infrastructure are made available, including external resources; and

b. Dedicated resources to better understand clients and markets are provided.

*3. People*

a. Roles and responsibilities are clearly defined;

b. Appropriate people are utilized in project teams;

c. Outside resources can be utilized;

d. Cross-team activity is facilitated;

e. Project participants are not penalized for the time spent on such initiatives; and

f. Failures as well as successes are celebrated.

It is worth noting that, of all the qualities needed to successfully innovate, "commitment of top management" was seen as the single most important requirement by respondents to Boston Consulting Group's 2013 Innovation Leaders Survey.[2] The need for the leadership team to devote the necessary time was also seen by as the third most important requirement in the same survey out of a list of 17 possibilities.

## The stage-gate process in detail

### The Innovation Proposal Template

I have set out below the suggested format for an Innovation Proposal Template, which any project team could use when seeking initial review and support at Stage 1. I do not suggest that it should be entirely completed prior to Stage 1; in fact, it is better that this does not happen so the innovation committee can give some guidance on its completion.

The template anticipates many of the issues which will need to be addressed as the proposal advances through the various "gates", while, in the initial stages, it at least gives the innovation committee an overview of what the proposal is about so that the detailed requirements of Stage 1 can be addressed.

## Innovation Proposal Template

| | |
|---|---|
| Project name | |
| Team members | |
| Sponsor | |
| Date submitted | |

| | |
|---|---|
| Brief description of aims of project | |

## Key criteria

| | |
|---|---|
| Does the project meet the firm's qualifying criteria? | |

| | Topic | Response | Guide |
|---|---|---|---|
| 1. | The "idea" will: | | Focus on the client's perspective and need to "make gain or avoid pain". Does the solution fit with the client's business model and priorities? |
| | Solve what problem? | | |
| | Offer what benefit? | | |
| | Get what specific job done? | | |
| | Create what opportunity for the client or the firm? | | |
| (Leave next section blank if the innovation is designed for internal firm use only) | | | |
| 2. | Who would pay us for providing such a solution? | | |
| | Amongst our current client base? | | Try to identify specific clients or markets with common requirements |
| | In a potential new market? | | Could it create a new market? A market in a different state/region or country? |

| | Topic | Response | Guide |
|---|---|---|---|
| | Identify/describe an "ideal" potential client for this service/product | | This does not have to be a current client |
| | Does such an idea fit with any current services/products offered by us? | | Would it be purchased in conjunction with another service or be a "stand-alone"? |
| (If innovation is purely for internal use, complete the following section as though references to "market" and "client" refer to internal users of proposed innovation) | | | |
| 3. | Proof of concept | | |
| | How would you test the nature and size of the market to which this idea might have appeal? | | This should include client interviews, market research, pilot schemes and the creation of a "minimum viable product" (i.e. something realistic on which client reaction can be assessed). |
| | Who might be able to assist? | | |
| | Estimate how long and what resources (time and money) you might need to validate your idea | | |
| | Identify key assumptions you have made which must be validated if the project is to succeed | | This might include the size of the potential market, the usefulness of the idea, its pricing, timing, funding, staffing etc. |
| 4. | Competing or similar solutions | | |
| | Can you identify any competing or similar solutions that are in the market currently? | | Consider not only our industry but any other industry |
| | Does your idea compliment or compete with any other similar idea being advanced within the firm? | | Check with your sponsor |

| | Topic | Response | Guide |
|---|---|---|---|
| 5. | The firm | | |
| | Does your idea fit with what you understand are the firm's strategic priorities? | | Discuss with your sponsor to clarify |
| | If realized, do you see the implementation of your idea having any negative impacts on the firm? Would it require major changes within the firm? | | Will your idea undermine existing services or products being offered by the firm? Why might your idea meet resistance from within the firm? |
| | What else could the firm do to assist you bring this idea to reality? | | Consider any additional points you wish to add to those already made above |

The aim of this document is to give the innovation committee as much information as early as possible to assist you in every way it can.

If you are having any difficulty completing any part of this submission, check with your sponsor.

*Figure 3: An Innovation Proposal Template*

*A version of this chapter was first published in Hart, D.,* Lean Innovation for Lawyers: Creating and Delivering an Innovation Strategy, *London, ARK Group, 2015*

## References

1. Ries, E., *The Lean Startup: How Today's Entrepreneurs Use Contiuous Innovation to Create Radically Successful Businesses*, Crown Business, New York, 2011.
2. Hart, D., *Lean Innovation for Lawyers: Creating and Delivering an Innovation Strategy*, London: ARK Group, 2015 (See: Chapter 11).
3. Boston Consulting Group, 'The Most Innovative Companies 2013', available at: www.bcgperspectives.com/content/articles/innovation_growth_most_innovative_companies_2013_lessons_from_leaders/#chapter1.

# Chapter 5: Succession planning – Ensuring losing a partner doesn't mean losing a client

*By Carol Mynott, director at PWC*

If the owner of a factory which produces widgets knows that the machinery used for production has a typical lifespan of 10 years, senior management will plan to bring a replacement online well before the 10 years is up. Why is it that I see firms all too often not plan for a partner retiring until the final few months? This runs the risk of rushing the handover and potentially losing the client. As businesses that create success based on the capability of its people and their relationships with clients, succession planning is critical to the long term sustainability of any law firm.

Over the last five years we've seen equity partner headcount in the Top 10 and Top 11-25 UK firms grow by only 7 percent over the five years to 2016. With most partnerships dominated by baby-boomers, it's not unusual to find firms where over half the partners are due to retire in the next five years. Particularly as many firms have a forced retirement age between 60 and 65. Planning for this kind of sweeping senior turnover would be important in any industry. But in a people-and-relationship based business like legal services, being prepared fully for it is imperative.

## What should firms do to start to future-proof themselves?

A managing partner once said to me "It's part of every partner's role to identify high-performing talent, both employees and other partners, to help them build and develop their skills to grow with the firm. The challenge I have is getting my partners to understand this and then to act on it".

So how should firms start when planning for partner retirements and broader succession planning? The two key areas I've focused on in this article are culture and building a plan.

## Culture

Changing the culture within a firm isn't something that can be done by publishing a vision and set of values on a website. Culture comes from the everyday small interactions between people. Here are the key building blocks needed to develop a culture to support succession planning:

- **True support from the top**: As succession planning is critical for business it is vital that the process is owned and run from the top of the firm. It can't be a HR initiative. HR are important in supporting the process and developing an approach to develop talent. Having real buy-in from the Board and time spent by them developing and executing the succession plan sets the tone for the firm and sends a message to the rest of the partnership about how important this is.
- **Define the role of a partner in the years coming up to retirement**: The primary role of a partner is to generate revenue, but in the years before retirement what you actually want is for a partner to bring in *less* revenue – and to allow others to step in and take up the strain (and billable hours) before they go. Typically partners are reluctant to talk about planning for future retirement with a fear of how they will be perceived by their peers. Clearly defining the role of a pre-retirement partner can help to make this transition period a requirement as opposed to behind closed doors. This openness gives senior partners time to provide support and direction while junior partners get to grips with the new role and develop their skills. I have a management consulting client who requires partners to reduce their work activity over the last two years as they work towards retirement. This requires them to drop to an 80 percent week and then to a 50 percent week. This allows the partner to pass on their skills and client relationships but also to start developing links and skills for their role after leaving the firm, such as non-executive director roles or working with charities. In this example the partner's reward is reduced over the two years but not to the same extent as the time reduction. This then creates funds to pay for a new partner to be to be promoted into the partnership while the senior partner is still working with them.
- **New approach to remuneration and incentives to develop others**: Succession planning fails when there is no incentive for partners to mentor their people. The traditional approaches to assessing partner performance and partner reward decisions pay very little attention to this. The fundamental area of focus is on

current revenue with very little focus on what the partner is doing to develop long-term sustainable revenue growth, not just by developing client relationships and propositions but also in how they have grown two or more people who might succeed them. Metrics along these lines need to be brought in to help to incentivise partners through the firm to focus on succession planning.

- **Diversity**: Trying to put an identical replacement into every role is almost certain to be the wrong approach. When I mention diversity I'm not just referring to gender or ethnicity. It is about people who think, work, and maybe act differently – who bring a different perspective to a client problem to help further enhance the service delivered. Succession planning needs to include steps to actively promote "difference" for leadership opportunities as well as training partners to have an open mind to this. It is human nature to seek people who are like oneself for mentoring and promotion but each firm needs to challenge this.
- **Don't just look in the obvious places**: It is all too easy to assume that the successor to a partner in a key client relationship role is the person who directly reports to that partner today. I've seen examples where this really hasn't worked as the number two just doesn't have the right skills to lead the whole relationship. This means that the net needs to be cast wider. Is there someone on a different client account who might be better suited? How about from a different practice group? Or maybe in a different part of the world?
- **Communication**: How often have you heard of someone resigning from a firm, only to be told at that moment that they were part of its top talent and earmarked for great things? If only they'd been told this earlier, they might have stuck around. Having open and honest conversations about the potential we see in candidates and the opportunities which might be open to them helps to dispel any assumptions or myths. The lack of a clear plan can lead to unease on both sides. Having these conversations can be daunting at first but I've found that both the individual and the firm can benefit.

## How to build a succession plan

From my experience of working with clients planning for a smooth "changing of the guard" there are six areas of focus:

1. **Understanding the strategic priorities of the firm**: Using the firm's strategy as a starting point provides clarity about which areas of the firm are more important to consider than others. This also helps to make sure resources can be allocated appropriately.
2. **Identify the most vital roles in the firm**: The key here is to identify critical roles rather than critical people. The obvious roles include the managing partner and members of the senior leadership team as they're important to the running of the business, but more critically will be the roles of those holding key client relationships, fundamental technical capabilities, or in growth areas. To use an army story from a friend of mine, while the British troops were in Afghanistan some of the most critical roles were those of the communications experts – if the enemy took the communication channels out this could debilitate the whole group so having a specialist who could fix this as quickly as possible was far more important than the most senior officer.
3. **What skills might we need in the future**: Using the past can help inform the future but it can't always be relied upon to accurately predict what will happen. The way that working in professional services is changing at such a relentless pace means that when considering each business critical role we need to consider how the skills might need to be different in the future. Alongside this we also need to consider future roles which may not be present today.
4. **"Mind the gap"**: This is where succession planning really starts to create value – understanding where there are gaps in capability today but also assessing possible future gaps. An honest assessment of the strengths, skills, and goals of not just your high performing partners but all partners helps the firm to compare the needs of current and future roles with the capabilities within the firm. Firms can then decide what needs to be done to be ready. This might be to bring "new blood" from outside the firm or to move a high-performing senior associate to retrain in a new area/territory to ensure they progress to partner and fill the gap in time without running the risk of taking a chance on a lateral hire. In actual fact there are many schools of thought who believe that leaders developed from within the organization tend to be more successful than those brought in from outside.
5. **Development of skills and those acting as mentors**: Now that you know who might be right for future succession and the skills

they need to develop, this is where individual partners should create individual development plans to define how they build the relevant skills. This might be by attending a formal training programme or in a more informal way by moving the partner to develop those skills on the job. An example might be if a partner has the potential to be a practice group leader, they may develop their leadership skills by running a smaller business team first. This also helps to understand where potential "bottlenecks" may cause a problem for the individual developing their skills. For example, where immediate senior partners are likely to stay in a role for some time and limit the progression of the individual. Knowing where the bottlenecks are likely to be helps firms to plan for these and prevent losing key talented individuals. Sometimes even a sideways move may be an alternative way of gaining additional experience to then move on to a more senior role. While we're on the topic of skills development, we should also consider the ability of senior partners to coach and mentor other partners. We shouldn't just assume that they are able to do this. This may mean that training and maybe additional support is needed for senior partners to make sure they do this effectively.

6. **Time commitment needed from senior leadership**: If succession planning is done properly it can lead to significant savings for the firm as the need for lateral hires to be parachuted in becomes rare. But what it does require is time from leadership. They need to spend the time understanding the roles and the candidates as well as helping to coach and support them. This commitment also clearly needs role models for the partner group to demonstrate that this is business critical and then they should start to follow suit.

Building a succession plan isn't just about putting some names in boxes and then filing the document. It needs real investment and this will take time and there will be some hurdles along the way. Partners need to be accountable for developing junior partners and creating room for them to hone their skills so that they are ready for the next challenge for them to reach their full potential. If this doesn't happen then this needs to be recognized. For some firms, going through a process like this can be daunting which means they never get started but this can be overcome by piloting with a specific practice group or territory – once other areas of the firm see the positive effects succession planning can have then they will want to get involved.

Coming back to my point at the beginning, succession planning is a business imperative for all legal firms. Any partner who's nearing retirement and has the long-term interests of the firm at heart should be happy to share and pass on relationships and knowledge. A core principle of joining a partnership is that you should strive to leave it in a better place than when you joined: and any partner who isn't prepared to do this is actually failing in his or her duties.

# Chapter 6:
# Compensation to reward the right behaviors

*By Arthur G. Greene, principal at Boyer Greene LLC*

Compensation systems are often a reflection of what firm founders thought made sense at one point in time. While the firms have undergone change over the years, the original compensation systems are likely embedded in the firm culture. Unfortunately, law firms have a tendency to avoid reconsidering their compensation systems, even if they are outdated and becoming increasingly contentious.

As the legal marketplace has become more challenging, the compensation process in successful law firms has evolved into a management tool. The concept in this new approach is both simple and logical. Compensation systems should reward desired behaviors and penalize unwanted behaviors. Not only does this approach ensure that every lawyer is working for what is best for the firm, it also avoids the troublesome process of trying to decide an individual's "fair compensation" in a vacuum.

The groundwork involved in using compensation as a management tool starts by identifying the goals of the firm and the lawyer behaviors required in order for the firm to achieve those goals. While each lawyer's contribution may be different, they are rewarded based on the extent to which their contribution advances the goals and objectives of the firm. The difference between individual success and firm success is front and center in this discussion.

## What are the desired behaviors?

A law firm expects all of its lawyers to be competent, ethical, and to have good practice management skills. Beyond those basic characteristics, there are a range of other skills that will be deemed desirable, but no firm wants every lawyer to be the same. It takes a mix of talents and skills for a firm to achieve success. All essential skills should be identified and rewarded based on their relative value to the firm.

## Revenue production

Every compensation system will include revenue production at the top of the list of behaviors to be rewarded. However, do not make the mistake of limiting compensation rewards to raw individual dollar production. Productivity in law firms means more than that. Lawyers need to be rewarded for:

- The dollars leveraged by delegating work to associates and paralegals;
- The profitability of work as measured by realization rates; and
- Originating work that can be transferred to other partners.

Partners who manage and supervise the work of associates and paralegals are contributing more to the firm than partners who work on their own matters in isolation. The profitability of the work performed is also a critical factor. Revenue produced has to be analyzed in light of the billable hours used to achieve those fees. And finally, do not underestimate the value of the partner who is producing clients that are transferred to other partners who may be having trouble developing a full book of business.

Partners will try to conduct themselves in ways that will make them look good on the financial reports. A prime example of a missed opportunity, seen in many small and mid-sized firms, is the reporting of individual hours worked and dollars produced categorized by partners, associates, and paralegals.

If the partners do not get dollar credit for the hours worked by the associates and paralegals working on their files, management is sending a signal that delegation is not encouraged. The result is partners tend to hoard work to make their numbers look good, thereby causing associates to be underutilized. This is a classic example of incentivizing the wrong behavior.

To incentivize delegation, firms need to give significant weight to the column in the financial reports called "Responsible attorney" (or "Billing attorney") under which each partner's credit includes the dollars generated by the associate and paralegal work they manage. To incentivize profitable work, there should be a column entitled "Realization rate". To incentivize referrals to other partners, there should be a column entitled "Transfer credits".

Reports considered critical in today's law firms include:

- Billable hours – by partners and associates;
- Billings – by responsible attorney;
- Collections – by responsible attorney;
- Realization rate (profitability) – by responsible attorney;
- Aged work-in-process – by responsible attorney;
- Aged collections – by responsible attorney; and
- Transfer credits (originations transferred) – by partner transferring clients to other partners.

Most firms focus on the responsible attorney as the best means for assuring accountability with regard to the effective use of firm resources. It holds the partner who manages the matter responsible for associate and paralegal time with regard to any write-offs or uncollected fees.

#### Subjective contributions

There are also important non-financial contributions that are critical to the success of a law firm. For example, a subjective compensation system typically recognizes and rewards a number of factors, including:

- Successfully promoting the goals and objectives of the firm;
- Mentoring young lawyers;
- Assisting others in the firm, quietly and without fanfare; and
- Leading in the community and/or the bar associations.

There are always some partners who seem to make larger contributions to the goals and objectives of the firm than others. The reference may be to the partner who is the "glue" that holds the firm together and/or keeps it on course. Another factor defying an objective measurement is the elusive contribution of being a positive influence on the firm's culture. Or, it can be a matter of helping others, such as mentoring associates or selflessly assisting other partners in time of need. The term "team player" is a classic description.

#### Leadership and management

Strong positive leadership and effective management can make all the difference in a law firm's success. The founders of successful law firms are usually effective in leading and managing; it is the transition to the next generation that can be problematic. Compensation systems need to incentivize and reward:

- Being an effective leader in the firm; and
- Contributing to the management of the firm.

Effective leadership may come from those partners who can in their own distinctive way contribute significantly to the consensus and direction of the firm efforts. Leadership can be highly visible, or quiet, effective leadership by example.

**Recognizing the need for a change in determining compensation**

There is no issue more important, more delicate, and potentially more destructive than partner compensation. Undertaking a change can seem risky based on the uncertainties involved. On the other hand, maintaining a system that is not rewarding desired behaviors and/or has become contentious can do serious damage to the future success of the firm.

A partner compensation system probably needs to be re-evaluated if it:

- Is not well understood by the partners;
- Is overly complex;
- Is not considered credible and fair;
- Does not involve open and candid discussions;
- Fails to reward desired behaviors;
- Rewards unwanted behaviors;
- Allows partners to "game" the system;
- Puts the success of the individual ahead of the success of the firm;
- Creates an unhealthy tension among the partners;
- Causes excessive internal competitions;
- Results in disruption or distraction; or
- Gives little to no hope for the aspiring associate.

Having a partner compensation system that works for the firm in all respects will be critical to its success, particularly in these more competitive times.

Consider the following examples of problematic scenarios that are not serving the firm's long term interests:

**The small firm with a formula-based system**

The firm's partners are between the ages of 58 and 74. The firm has employed associates but they were always underutilized and complained of a lack of opportunity for career development. Partners are not rewarded for mentoring or training associates and find it easier and quicker to do the work themselves. Turnover has been high with no associate ever approaching the point of candidacy for partnership. The partners are approaching retirement age, there is no second generation of lawyers to serve the firm's ongoing clients, and there is no realistic exit plan for any of the partners. Partners will miss out on receiving any rewards for the practices they built.

**The mid-sized firm with a complicated system**

The firm has 23 partners and nine associates. The partners' compensation system is based on a formula set up by the founders in 1964. There have been adjustments and additions to the system, which only the bookkeeper understands. While there is both a formula part and a subjective part to the analysis, the partners are not energized or incentivized because they do not understand how their behaviors affect their compensation. The firm as a whole is feeling stagnant and its future is in doubt.

**The mid-sized firm with the "old boys" in control**

The firm has 15 partners and seven associates. The partner compensation system is divided into three columns:

- Formula-based;
- Subjective; and
- Seniority-based.

A significant portion of the profit is divided based on the seniority column where the five senior partners hold most of the points. No seniority points are available for allocation to others unless or until one of the current members of that group retires. Two of the senior members holding significant points are not productive and a number of the younger partners are undercompensated. The firm is unable to attract laterals and the firm's most highly rated associate resigned after being offered a partnership.

These are extreme but actual scenarios to show the dangers that arise from continuing with compensation systems that are archaic. These scenarios are also intended to demonstrate the risks to each firm's long term success.

## Introducing incentives

The next question involves how to incorporate appropriate incentives into existing compensation systems that are not now incentive-based. Firms with subjective systems have a distinct advantage over firms that are strictly formula-based. Part of any firm's analysis should include whether it is time for the firm to abandon an outdated system in favor of a newly constructed incentive-based subjective system focused on the success of the firm as an institution.

## Compensation systems

Typically, the smallest law firms are first-generation firms. Two or more lawyers started the firm with a compensation arrangement that met their immediate needs, but did not contemplate growth of the firm. Many of these start-up firms relied on some type of formula-based system. While the system adopted by the founders often worked well for a time, they began to work less well as additional partners were added to the firm.

The law firms with the most troubled compensation systems are in the mid-sized range. A good example would be firms that have experienced rapid growth but are burdened by the compensation system established by the founders when the firms were established. They may be struggling to maintain the founders' original compensation system, even though it may have become increasingly contentious. The partners may be tolerating a poorly-operating system rather than risk the unknown that change would bring. Often these archaic systems are not incentivizing the right behaviors, but rather are rewarding individual successes. These firms are at a crossroads and desperately need to evaluate and revamp their compensation system.

Large firms tend to have settled into some type of subjective compensation system that has caused the firm to succeed and endure from one generation to the next. Minor changes may have been made, from time to time, in order to adjust to changing circumstances, either in the firm or the marketplace. These firms need to re-evaluate the details of their systems and be certain that they update their incentives as needed.

## Incentivizing behaviors under different systems

Most compensation systems in law firms today fall into one of three general categories:

- Formula systems;
- Subjective systems; or
- Combination systems.

There are an unlimited number of variations within each category, leading to the assumption that no two systems are exactly alike.

### Formula-based systems

Incentivizing behaviors in a formula-based system is a challenge. Inherent in a formula system is the overriding concept that an individual's compensation is tied directly to revenue generation. Any effort to incentivize other behaviors is both logistically difficult and contrary to the underlying purpose of the system. Because of the strict focus on revenue generation, these firms tend to lack good management, mentoring of associates, teamwork, succession, etc. While a formula-based firm can achieve short term success, they rarely remain successful into a second generation.

In order to broaden the incentives beyond the revenue generation, the question becomes whether to incorporate elements of subjective evaluations into the formula or to evolve to an actual subjective system. It is telling that the vast majority of successful second generation mid-sized and large firms operate with some type of subjective system.

In order to motivate at least one of the lawyers to volunteer to be managing partner, some firms with formula-based systems provide for additional lump-sum payments to partners taking on that role. The results of this approach are mixed. Some formula-based firms have moved in the direction of a combination system which includes a formula component and a subjective component. A first step is often to identify a percentage of the firm's distributable profits (or a predetermined lump-sum) to be set aside and distributed subjectively based on non-revenue producing contributions to the success of the firm. Again, results are mixed. These efforts to undercut the original intent of a formula system seem to result in a confused and controversial process. It is nearly impossible to get around the definitional focus that a formula-based system is intended to reward income generation.

### Subjective systems

Subjective compensation systems are the most common, particularly among mid-sized firms with an institutional approach to success. In such a system the partners identify the factors that are to be considered in setting compensation. A committee is usually responsible for evaluating individual contributions and recommending compensation in the form of points. Subjective compensation systems are sometimes referred to as "rough justice", recognizing that contributions to the success of the firm cannot be effectively reduced to an exact number.

In a subjective system, the committee gives weight to billable hours, leveraging through delegation, billings, billing realization, collections, collection realization, transfer credits, etc. These data points are considered subjectively, meaning no math is undertaken to determine the relative contribution of any partner. The other significant difference is that the committee considers subjective factors beyond revenue production, such as the partner's contribution to management, to the training and mentoring of associates, and to teamwork, as well as a variety of other ways the partner contributes to the overall success of the firm. The weight applied to the various factors is also a subjective consideration.

The key ingredients in a successful subjective system include:

- An agreement as to the factors to be considered;
- A deliberate and careful evaluation of each partner's contributions; and
- Clear communication to each partner as to the basis of his or her compensation amount.

A firm with a subjective compensation system is well positioned to analyze whether it is rewarding desired behaviors, and making changes as appropriate.

## Conclusion

Law firms are under constant change imposed by both their clients and the legal marketplace. The most successful firms are those that have been most effective in recognizing and responding to these needs for change.

While a partner compensation system can seem like an internal matter isolated from marketplace concerns, this is not the case. An outdated and/or contentious partner compensation system can result in serious consequences which can undermine other efforts to remain competitive and successful. For firms planning on succession, it is essential to have a fair and efficient compensation system in place to attract desirable laterals and ambitious associates.

All partners need to be focused on the goals and objectives of the firm and be rewarded based on how well they advance the interests of the firm. This involves having a compensation system that incentivizes the behaviors required to meet the challenges and prevail in challenging times, as well as position the firm well for the future.

*A version of this chapter was first published in Darcy, S., (ed.)* Compensation (Re)Design for Law Firms, *London, ARK Group, 2016*

# Chapter 7: Changing minds – The neuroscience of change management in law firms

*By Nick Marson, CEO of The Parallel Mind*

For managing partners, leading change in the new legal age is hard. It is easy to get stuck and to feel overwhelmed. However, neuroscience research can be used to give you new perspectives on leading change.

Despite all of our technological advances, the brain is primitive. It weighs about 1.4 kilograms and has a minimum of 900 billion brain cell connections called neurons, each with more than 1,000 contacts (synapses) with other neurons. It produces 25 watts of electricity a second (equivalent to a small light bulb).

The next stage in human evolution will be expanded conscious awareness. Your brain consists of your unconscious basal ganglia, deep in the centre of your brain, and your conscious thinking, the prefrontal cortex at the front of your head. This is where your mind resides, your conscious awakening.

Your unconscious mind, or basal ganglia, is a collection of mechanisms that perform the vital autopilot functions that keep you alive. It regulates your heartbeat, breathing, and repetitive motor movements like walking. It sends a million little scouts to survey the landscape and report back, storing most of what it encounters and processing up to a million bits of information a second.

The conscious mind, by contrast, is far more selective. It can only pay attention to a maximum of four things at a time, so choose carefully. Immediate memory can only remember up to seven items at a time, with three being the optimal number.

## Intentions vs behavior

There is a gap between our conscious intentions and our unconscious behaviour. The unconscious mind is hardwired to resist change. It is a lot bigger and stronger than the conscious mind and has been honed over millions of years of evolution. Our brains are driven by basic responses towards pleasure or away from pain, based on external stimuli processed by the limbic system or emotional centre of the brain. When it senses a threat, the amygdala hijacks our conscious brains. This primitive knee-jerk reaction puts us in automatic fight or flight model; we are hijacked by fear which often isn't rational.

There are three things you can do to lead minds in the direction you want to take them:

1. Set a clear direction;
2. Motivate unconscious minds; and
3. Clear the path.

When the unconscious and conscious parts of the brain are working together in harmony, a powerful dual processor core creates optimal performance.

Being humble and setting the right leadership tone puts people at ease and reduces the status threat inherent in law firms. Providing clear communication of expectations helps to increase certainty. Letting others take charge and make decisions increases their autonomy.

The real skill of the managing partner is to lead without appearing to lead. Being authentic, a real person, creates a sense of personal connection and relatedness. By being open and transparent and listening to their followers, natural leaders create a sense of fairness that builds personal trust.

## Embracing change

Our brains are naturally hardwired to resist change. Our unconscious emotional brains crave safety. So, to embrace change, you have to focus your conscious brain.

First, you need to have the intention to do something. Then, you need to pay attention to what you want to do. Next, you need to do it. Then, repeat the process.

Attention density changes the brain. Every time you pay attention to something, the neurons in your brain fire and your neural paths rewire. The brain is plastic, wired to change to meet the challenges of a constantly-changing environment. But if you want to be in charge, you need to be mindful.

Attention is the key that unlocks your free will; it is the gatekeeper to your awareness. Consciousness acts as a "bright spot" on the stage, directed by the selective spotlight of attention.

Mindfulness can activate wilfully-directed attention. For Buddhists, it is the moment of restraint that allows mindful awareness to take hold and deepen. Directed mental force stops the grinding machines of the unconscious. Mindfulness is falling awake, getting out of your own way and paying attention in the moment.

## Building relationships

> ***"I've learned that people will forget what you said, people will forget what you did, but people will never forget how you made them feel."***
>
> Maya Angelou

We are wired to be social. Our default network in the brain is social. We are driven by relationships. When our brains are relaxed, we start thinking of ourselves and other people in our social networks. We are social animals, strongly dependent on our social standing in our social groups to survive and thrive.

Circuitry has been recently discovered in the brain that lets us tune into and resonate emotionally with each other during a face-to-face interaction. Video conferences can't replicate this human connectedness so, if it is really important, get on that plane.

Your social brain is a mirror. The important discovery of mirror neurons that fire when we witness another person's suffering gives a scientific basis to empathy. Without this ability to feel empathy and compassion, human beings would simply not be able to cooperate. Empathy is the basis of rapport and trust. Mirror neurons create the personal closeness that builds relationships.

Empathic concern is a key attribute of successful leaders. Empathic literacy, explicit understanding of what someone else feels and thinks at any given moment, is the key skill for leaders of change.

We are emotional beings. Your primitive limbic system is in control and coats everything with emotional significance. You cannot make a rational decision without first getting an emotional response from your emotional brain. Every time we think, we are being influenced by feelings based on our emotional experiences.

According to the Institute of Heart Math, neural networks are contained in the cardinal sack. So we really do see from the heart.

## Improving learning

Your brain is a self-organizing emergent system. Every day, hundreds of thousands of synapses are released into the brain as a free-learning resource to make new connections. The brain is constantly adapting to a changing environment in search of wholeness, to find a natural order.

Learning is an emotional experience; we learn best when we are engaged. The hippocampus, responsible for memory, sits inside the limbic system, the emotional centre of the brain.

Optimal learning is a social activity; we learn best when we are in small groups. So, leaders should create a multitude of informal opportunities for followers to learn together.

## Importance of insight

Having powerful insights changes the brain and releases dopamine pleasure molecules and little hits of oxytocin, the reward chemical of the brain. This happens in the anterior cingulate cortex, the brain region for detecting novelty. When we have an insight, the brain oscillates in the gamma band – the fastest brain frequency waves – at forty times a second.

Insight is central to long-term change, but each person needs to have their own insight and not just listen to their leader's insight. To encourage thinking, leaders need to ask questions with the word "think" in them. Attention drives change and is the active ingredient for changing the brain.

A leader's job is to help others to think better for themselves.

## Leading change

In the new legal age, emergent leadership will be the new paradigm. Holding the emerging space for others to think better will be a key skill. Your ability to lead others may well depend on your ability to lead yourself. To consciously intervene, do things in a timely and mindful way. In essence, develop a greater level of cognitive control.

Observing your own thoughts is central to your ability to choose between the active and the passive, to switch from autopilot to taking control. Being more present and self-aware, in the moment, leads to a state of "letting come", allowing you to consciously participate in a larger field of change.

Honing your ability to observe your inner experience, to think about your thinking, to see what you're seeing, to imagine different futures, to connect the dots in search of wholeness and, above all to be mindful, will be the future leader's way.

*A version of this article first appeared in* Managing Partner *in 2014.*

# Chapter 8: Getting commitment to change

*By Alicia Fortinberry and Bob Murray, principals at Fortinberry Murray*

**In this chapter we look at:**

- Why people resist change;
- The assumptions that create resistance;
- The use, and misuse, of influencers;
- How to overcome resistance in individuals and firms; and
- How to make change stick.

Many consultants and other gurus claim that people should "embrace change" as if that were something that you could do simply by trying. Their pontifications have found a special place in the hearts of some law firm leaders. "All I need to do", the managing partner of a mid-sized US law firm told us just before a presentation we gave at the Mid-Western Law Forum conference a couple of years ago, "is to get the partners to embrace change – to see that the changes I'm suggesting are good for them".

The pity of it is that humans don't work that way. They do not generally accept change because it is "good for them" – otherwise every child would eat their greens and no adult would smoke or drink to excess. I fear that this managing partner would have remained disappointed.

However, all is not lost. Humans do not like to change, but they can be *persuaded* to, and recent discoveries in human science show how this can be done. This chapter is about how to get people genuinely to commit to change and also how to make change successful. We'll be looking at the latest science in the area of change and suggesting ways to get around the knee-jerk resistance that we all have to it.

## Why people resist change

Resistance to change is inbuilt; it's in our genes and in our neurobiology. The neural pathways that any call to change goes through are the same ones that carry messages about physical and emotional pain. Change can make us ill, both mentally and physically. Any change which threatens to affect a person's life in a major way can cause the system to overproduce the kind of neurochemicals (principally cortisol) which, in excess, can cause major mental and physical illness. Those that look at the context – particularly the social context – of change, have pointed out that anything that threatens to change a person's network of relational support (family, office, friendships) causes potentially damaging stress.[1]

When you, as a law leader, ask your people to make a change that is going to affect them in ways which threaten to alter their social context, you are asking them to put their health, and possibly their life, at risk. It's not the way corporate or firm CEOs – with their eyes on the balance sheet and the profit and loss figures – normally think. As a leader, your social context may not be threatened by the changes – in fact, if your social network is largely other law leaders, others in your C-suite, or corporate CEOs or political leaders, you may not be in any serious way affected by the change. You do not see the potential damage your brilliant new ideas may cause.

Any leader contemplating any significant change must realize that the greatest fear that humans have is of exclusion, or a fundamental disruption of their social relationships. Any change which threatens that will cause problems which will render the change initiative difficult at best. The threat of unemployment is harmful largely because it means exclusion from, perhaps, our main social nexus.

Although this is true for both sexes, it is truer for men than women.[2] Again, this is genetic. Men are wired to get their greatest social connection from those that they hunt with. Women tend to bond with a greater circle of people and have the ability to build vibrant social support systems outside of the work tribe. They have a greater neural ability to expand their connections. Retirement, or the threat of being laid off, is neurogenetically harder for men than women. However, as with men, women's sense of self-worth may be tied up with their career, and they may fear that losing a job may hinder their acceptance by their wider social network.

TOP TIP

**When planning for change, take people's fear of social change into account. Emphasize continuity of relationships.**

## The assumptions that create resistance

In times of change, both leaders and those they lead are blinded by their assumptions, most of which are wrong, but all of which are based on their genes and their experience. Unconsciously, most of us assume that others believe the same things we do, and that there's something wrong with them if they don't. We feel that our assumptions and beliefs are the "natural" and "rational" ones to have about any situation.

However, other than a belief such as that 1+1=2, there are no rational beliefs. Your assumption, for example, that "digitizing our knowledge management will benefit the firm" is not a rational belief like 1+1=2. Rather, it is built upon a foundation of your experience and your genome.

You say, "look at the facts", or "look at the savings", or "look at the increase in efficiency", and you are just looking at what you are predisposed to look at. You are not looking at what the other person is looking at, the things that matter to them: their fears, their assumptions, and their motivations.

### Assumptions based on biology

What you are predisposed to look at is often governed by the non-rational parts of your biology, by your genetic inheritance. Here are some examples.

#### *1. You are probably genetically inclined to be a leader*

About 40 percent of all leaders have the same expression of a particular cluster of genes that dispose a person to either be a leader or a follower.[3] In terms of genetics, this is a high correlation. You will see the world from the perspective of that genetic predisposition. Leaders with that genetic predisposition are more likely to insist that they are right and are unlikely to listen to contrary opinions, or if they do, to admit that they have any validity.[4]

CASE STUDY

A few years ago, we were brought in to help a mid-sized firm. The managing partner was a man in his early fifties who wanted to make the business more "client responsive". "It is so obvious", he told us, "that this is the virtue that the firm needs". We asked him what "client responsiveness" meant. "Every partner knows that", he answered in disbelief that we should ask such a silly question.

Later, we were doing a workshop for 15 of the firm's most senior partners and we asked them, anonymously, to write down what they thought it meant. Each one had a different answer from "being knowledgeable about the law" to "answering my mobile at all times".

Later, we showed the MP the answers. "They just don't get it", he said, with some annoyance. "Client responsiveness means taking the client to lunch and listening to his needs of our firm. Every partner should know that."

The result of the MP's fixed idea was that, to nearly all the partners and the senior associates, the very idea of being more responsive to clients became something of a joke. The tragedy was that becoming more responsive was exactly what the firm needed, and if the MP had had the ability to listen to his partners' ideas of what it meant, he would have found some great suggestions of behaviors to adopt, and a great deal of support.

### *2. You are genetically predisposed to be a risk taker, or not*

Risk takers are not generally aware that they are more willing to take a chance than others, and often are not able to take others' risk avoidance into consideration. Most leaders are risk takers; however, male leaders are generally more inclined to take risks involving the groups/firms they lead than female leaders.[5]

CASE STUDY

The board of a relatively large US firm had the job of finding a new CEO. The current holder of the post had been a consensus leader and had been inclined to take a "steady as she goes" approach to the challenges that he faced. Under his leadership, the business had grown steadily but without a great deal of innovation and there was a danger that other, more aggressive firms would begin to take a serious chunk of their market share.

The members of the board thought that a more dynamic leadership was called for and they decided – against our advice – to promote a man who had been the successful leader of one of their Asian branches. In that role, he had championed a number of innovations which the current CEO had thought too risky, and had vetoed. As soon as he took the post, the new man began to make changes and to champion a merger with another firm of roughly the same size. He wouldn't listen to those partners advising caution, and who claimed that the merger target was not a good fit. His assumption, which he wouldn't allow to be challenged, was that the risk was worth it and the rewards should be self-evident to all but the most timid. He dismissed those who opposed him as being "too fearful" or "too near sighted". A number of his best rainmakers felt sidelined and left.

Within five months, the deal had collapsed and he himself left for another firm. "If I'd had more support", he intoned to us, "all would've been fine. They just didn't see it." Maybe, but the truth was that he couldn't see their point of view as valid. To him, such risk-taking was an essential part of leadership and it was that assumption that led to resistance and, ultimately, to failure.

TOP TIP

**Ask yourself: How often do you listen to, or read, the opinions of people you disagree with?**

### Assumptions based on experience

Of course, all stakeholders in any change situation have their own set of irrational assumptions; it is part of being human. Many of these are based on early experiences: childhood events, parental attitudes, teachers' and classmates' behaviors, and the like. Each of these can lead to assumptions that can render change more difficult for the individuals and the firm. Other assumptions can be based on work or other adult experiences.

Of course, not all assumptions are either harmful or wrong. Statistically, 30 percent are correct and even those that are not may be very useful in protecting the self from harm.

CASE STUDY

All assumptions – good or bad, right or wrong – are simply learned coping mechanisms. For example, a senior partner in a major Magic Circle firm in the UK had a parent who only praised her for her excellence at academic achievement. As a result, she was head of her class at school and in the top 0.5 percent of her class each year at law school. She got a job at the firm based on her deep knowledge of the law and her passion to explore it further. Her assumption was that her worth lay in her understanding of the intricacies of the law, for which she was praised and for which she was promoted. She was the firm's foremost expert in her field.

However, times change. Law firms change priorities. Flexibility, commerciality, and entrepreneurship became the watchwords for her firm. She feared the loss of importance that her grasp of the law had brought her. She couldn't change. She was sidelined. There are many lawyers like her in most firms whose assumptions about themselves prevent them from coming to terms with the changing needs of clients.

The more you try to persuade these lawyers of the need to change, the more they may become entrenched in their assumptions – no matter how many times they mouth their agreement. The reason for this is that our assumptions and our beliefs are very often so entrenched that they become part of our sense of self, and any attempt by someone to directly contradict them becomes, in our subconscious, an attack on us personally.

## Overcoming resistance to change

However, as we said at the start, all is not lost. Humans do not like to change, but they can be persuaded to accept it, and recent discoveries in human science show how this can be done. Fear of social loss can be mitigated. Self-limiting assumptions, based on biology or experience, can be replaced by more enabling ones. But not by direct assault on a person's belief system or by giving them facts; both of these are often counter-productive.

In getting individuals or groups to change their behavior or their attitudes, there are two fundamental things to bear in mind and to act upon:

- Commitment to change is, in the end, commitment to you, or someone else, as a leader; and
- Commitment to lasting change can only be achieved if a person, or group, feels safe.

### Getting commitment to you

The neuroscience of change is a hotly debated subject and is tied in with the whole issue of free will. Let's just say that the jury is out on some of the key issues. We do know a lot about the motivation and the process of change. All parties to the debate agree that people don't alter their behaviors or their attitudes because they have become persuaded by the facts or the reasoning. These are merely the excuses for the alterations, which happen after the decision to change has been made.[6]

Rather, people change their behaviors in order to strengthen actual, or potential, supportive relationships. They will adopt the new behaviors to gain the desired support, even if they do not necessarily believe in them. Whether the decision to alter a particular behavior or set of behaviors is ultimately conscious or unconscious, deliberate or automatic is irrelevant to this discussion – thank goodness!

We do know that if those new behaviors lead to good outcomes (ones where they are neurochemically gifted with one of the powerful reward neurochemicals, dopamine or oxytocin) then their brain (principally the orbitofrontal cortex, just behind the ear) will alter a person's "mindset" to account for, or justify, the behavioral change. This is true whether the change is a partner moving from one firm to another or their devoting more time and effort to business development.

As a firm leader, or as a manager or supervisor at any level of a firm who needs to promote changes in attitudes or behaviors, the relationship that most people need to be committed to is the one with you. If people feel that they will get more support and protection from you if they change their ways, then they will probably do so – even if they disagree with you.

The relationship that causes the change may be an existing relationship or a potential one. Often, you as a firm leader may be like a presidential candidate: a rather distant figure with whom most employees, even partners in large firms, will never have a real relationship. People can still develop a potential relationship with you, which can be just as effective in getting commitment.

People vote for politicians essentially because their striatum, a part of the limbic system of the brain that deals with trust and relationships (as well as a range of other things), has formed the opinion that the politician will offer them safety, and in order to gain that safety they will cast their vote in their favor. The striatum decides that there is a potential relationship between the voter and the candidate.

This decision can be based on a number of things that have little to do with what the politician stands for. It could be because they are taller than the other candidates (people tend to trust taller people), or has a deeper voice (people trust deeper voices more), or went to a similar school, or came from a similar town, or came from the same class, or is of the same race or gender, or has the same name, or has a combination of these or other commonalities which engender trust.

Having a similar world outlook can also be important, but having sufficient other commonalities can cause a person to vote for a candidate whose views they would not, initially, support. They will either change their views to rationalize the vote or argue that "really" they and the candidate share the same "values" or "outlook".

Having, and emphasizing, commonality is a vital way of gaining what we call "tribal commitment". However, in conjunction with other parts of the system, the striatum has other ways of judging the value of a real or potential relationship. You can inspire commitment to you, and to the change you advocate, through your actions or your achievements. Essentially, this is what a good role model does.

This action-inspiration is essentially a visual thing – something that is witnessed.[7] You are appealing directly to one of the most important social parts of the brain, where empathy lies – the mirror system. This is located in the left inferior frontal gyrus (at the front of the brain, just behind the eye).

Empathy with someone engenders commitment, and thus behavior change in order to support them – especially if there are commonalities in place. As with commonalities, the action or the modeling must be relevant to the person for them to be inspired. Just role modeling hard dedicated work will not inspire someone who doesn't feel that is the way for them. Scoring a hundred goals will not inspire somebody who hates football. A good leader will take the time to find out what actions will really inspire their followers, not just assume that they already know.

TOP TIP

**What do you have in common with your workforce? How can you demonstrate it?**

### Looking for influencers

Over the last five years, it has been decided in marketing circles that one of the ways to get people to be aware of products is to get what are called "influencers" to promote them. A lot has been written on the subject, but little real research has been done. Influencers, the proponents of these marketing schemes assert, are leaders, just as you are.

The idea transferred to the workplace, and elaborate graphics are produced showing who is connected to whom. Those with the greatest number of connections are called the influencers. It is said that, collectively, they may have more influence in the firm than you have.

It has been estimated by Neil Farmer, in his rather infamous 2008 book, *The Invisible Organization*, that the top leadership – no matter how powerful the leaders are – has no more than 20 percent of the influencing ability available in the firm.[8] It makes sense, it would seem, to identify and convince these all-powerful influencers and have them work their magic on the rest of the firm.

However, recent research has cast a bit of cold water on the idea. The idea of influencers comes from marketing through social media. The marketers mapped the online networks of people and measured the clusters of contacts they had. Some subjects had many more significant contacts than others – more people read their posts, for example, or responded to their chats. By this means, the "influencers" spread information and, it was presumed, influence.

The idea spread to change programs in large businesses, including law firms. Convince the people that your partners and employees really listen to and all is well, the theory went. But, as a number of recent studies have shown, listening to and being influenced by are two quite different things. One of the more interesting findings of social media experts is that the so-called influence of influencers may be very short lived, certainly not long enough to change any ingrained behavior.[9] The other is that people tend to read the posts of people that they already agree with. In either case, no real change takes place.

The behavioral neurogenetic reason for this is simple: influencers may not be really or potentially part of people's support networks. People only change behavior to get closer to, or to appease, the nexus of those they want or need support from. The mass influencers are not tapping into that very powerful genetic driver that lies behind all real lasting change. This is not to say that mass influencers don't have some impact, only that it is brief and cannot be relied upon, except as a way of getting an initial message out.

### The real influencers

For an individual partner or employee, real influencers are friends or support network members, or even people that they would like to have as part of their support network, not casual contacts. A leader can make use of this by instituting a mentoring program involving those in the firm that members admire or look up to – whether they are directly "connected" to them or not. Importantly, this must take into account differing cultural norms as to whom people admire, and not assumptions based on the leader's own social milieu. For example, in the US these influencers might be the chief rainmakers among the partners. Just over the border in Canada, they might not be so admired.

The firm leader should make a point of getting these people personally committed to them, and thus to any changes they want to institute. The real influencers become the change champions, the mentors, and the coaches. They will do this in order to solidify their relationship with the leader. In this way, adopting the new behaviors becomes the way that a person solidifies their place as a member of the firm's tribe.

## Making change stick

Once people have made the commitment to a behavioral change, the trick is to make that change stick. There has to be an ongoing reward which the neurogenetic system recognizes. This system is extremely primitive and is common to all creatures that have a brain. It is also very, very powerful and is a key driver in almost all of our actions.

Technically, it is called the "mesolimbic dopamine reward system". It plays a vital role in keeping us functioning because it reinforces behaviors which, essentially, are good for us. Or rather, to be strictly accurate, were good for hunter-gatherers on the African savannah. When we do something which benefits either us personally or the group to which we belong, the nucleus accumbens (a part of the limbic system that controls the reward neurochemical dopamine) makes sure we feel a pleasurable sensation, or a sense of satisfaction. This reinforces the behavior which produced the reward. The actions become cemented as a habitual behavior in a part of the brain called the basal ganglia which stores these behaviors and directs many of our activities – such as the unconscious actions involved in driving a car to work.

As the famous Russian behaviorist Ivan Pavlov showed in the early years of the last century, the habit engrained by what we now know as a "dopamine reward" will remain even when the actual reward is withdrawn. This is the famous "Pavlovian reaction" or, more accurately, "classical conditioning". Although his theories and experiments have been refined many times since, they still form the basis of all behavioral change and learning theory.

The reward that makes new behaviors stick will vary from person to person and context to context – a reward that produces a change of behavior in your teenager might not work in the office, or vice versa. But although the particular rewards will vary, the most powerful ones fall into four specific categories. These are what we call the BASE (our own acronym) social drivers.[10] These are:

- Belonging;
- Acceptance;
- Status; and
- Self-esteem.

At first glance, some of these seem to be the same thing, but to the neurogenetic system they are crucially different.

**Belonging**

Belonging is the most powerful of all of the rewards, and has long been recognized as such.[11] As a hunter-gatherer, you could not survive outside of your supportive band; belonging was a life-or-death issue. Recent research has shown that most of our genetics are designed in some way to facilitate social belonging. We fear exclusion more than anything else – even death.[12] People need to feel that they belong to a mutually supportive tribe and you, as the leader, are the one to encourage this mutuality and offer belonging in return for specific behavior. In a hunter-gatherer band, observing the rituals and obeying the totems were the price of belonging. So it is with a modern law firm.

The most obvious manifestation of this is the set of "values" that most firms have instituted. The problem with many of these is twofold. Firstly, they do not come with a set of concrete behaviors that the partners, or others, are expected to abide by so they often become, like "client responsiveness" referenced above, or "excellence", effectively meaningless.

Secondly, often partners are seen to get away with not following them. This situation led the HR director of a major UK-based firm to tell us that the institution of values only showed up the toxic environment that existed in the business.

The behaviors associated with the values are the important factor, not the values themselves. When one large law firm we work with instituted a firm-wide behavioral charter based on the values of "trust", "respect", and "co-operation" (with a list of values, the fewer the better), management organized it so that the whole firm – from receptionists to senior partners – had a say in what the behaviors should be and a vote as to which ones should be put into the charter. A partner could not become a partner unless that individual subscribed to the values, and all existing partners were invited to sign, literally, onto the charter. Of 200 partners, 198 did so.

### Social acceptance

Social acceptance is the visible sign that a person belongs to the tribe. As a leader, you show acceptance through praise, acknowledgement, or monetary reward. You noticeably show the person and others that you have accepted that individual, or group of individuals, into your circle of support, that they belong.

Again, in most firms there is some sort of ritual when lawyers are admitted into the partnership. The problem is that this type of ritual is usually limited to those becoming partners, not to non-lawyers being promoted or hired into the firm. This creates a "them and us" mentality. A functional hunter-gatherer band is organized to give all of its members a sense of being accepted. Often, partners defend the status-quo by saying that they are the "owners" of the business, or that they are the fee-earners and therefore deserve more acceptance than others.

Going forward, the first argument will be less and less true; most firms are being corporatized and, anyway, a sense of ownership when you have hundreds, if not thousands, of partners is wishful thinking. Such an organization is, in reality, no more than a joint-stock company (which, anyhow, many law practices are becoming) in which the partners are shareholders. The second point is also outdated. Recent research has shown that all the members of a firm contribute to its revenue, a point that is often overlooked and which we will be discussing later in the book.

### Status

In a tribe status equals safety. We were on safari in Tanzania not long ago and one day, towards dusk, we witnessed the reaction of a pack of baboons to the approach of a pair of female lions on the hunt. The pack immediately ran to the nearest large tree and climbed up. Of course, the baboons knew, as we all do, that the big cats can climb trees. The interesting thing was that the higher status apes went to the top of the tree and the lower status ones were left with the lower branches, with the high possibility that they would be sacrificed to preserve the lives of those of superior status. Our guide informed us that this was how they normally arranged themselves at night.

Human packs are essentially no different, which is why a sense of status is so important to us. If we feel that we have some status within the organizational tribe, we feel we will be protected by the other members, especially by the tribal leadership. Many studies have shown that the need for social status is a major human driver. However, status does not necessarily equal rank or social position. An equal number have shown that the attainment of socioeconomic status, or hierarchical rank of themselves do not increase one's sense of life satisfaction. The sense of status that is important to human beings is relative to those immediately around you and with whom you have regular contact.[13]

If adopting a change of behavior leads to an increase in relative status, then the change will be more readily accepted. A respected leader like Gavin Bell, ex-managing partner of Freehills, or Cameron Jay Raines, joint CEO of DLA Piper, is someone we call "status rich". The respect, trust, and admiration that people have for such a leader gives them their status. As such, they are capable of bestowing status on others (you cannot give what you don't have). Usually, this is by giving their followers specific praise, public acknowledgement, or increased authority or autonomy.

CASE STUDY

We saw this in action at a US law firm where the CEO wanted to encourage his partners to form high-performing teams (HPTs) which would collaborate closely together and, to use his term, "hunt as a pack". Up until then, the partners had behaved more like, again to use his term, "sole practitioners sharing serviced offices", as is the case in many large US firms. With his senior management, he created a number of small, diverse teams of partners and associates and tasked them with:

- Seeking out new clients or reengaging old ones;
- Exploring and learning from the approaches that other firms had taken with those clients;
- Experimenting with these and other new business development approaches for those clients; and
- Exchanging knowledge they had gleaned with individual partners and other teams.

This strategy was not new or even rocket science, but it was a revolutionary tactic for his firm. He gave those teams that tried new and innovative ways of acquiring and retaining clients praise for their efforts and publicly acknowledged their innovations. The most successful teams were given added status as well as monetary reward. The result was increased income per partner over the firm as a whole as other teams learned from the successes of the best HPTs. They were similarly encouraged and rewarded, leading to a change in behavior throughout the firm.

Research conducted at the Big 4 accountancy firms has shown that when a partner or other employee is praised, acknowledged, or granted more autonomy by a respected leader, that person subconsciously creates for themselves what is known as an "identity script" in which they see themselves as having equal or more status than those around them. This solidifies the new behaviors that have allowed them to write the new script.[14]

### Self-esteem

At first sight, a sense of status and self-esteem may seem much the same thing, but there are some fundamental differences. Firstly, status is totally bestowed upon us by outside influences such as our job title, the brand of the firm we work for, the praise and acknowledgement we are given. Self-esteem is largely hard-wired into us by our genes – maybe about 60 percent according to recent studies.[15] The neurophysiology of our brain, and in particular the strength of the signals that travel between the medial prefrontal cortex (the area dealing with self-knowledge) and the ventral striatum, also affects our level of self-esteem.[16]

In the end, probably 20 percent or so of our sense of self-worth comes from environmental influences. In behavioral terms, that is an important percentage. Essentially, a human's sense of self-esteem rises from its biological base when people make them feel good about themselves. These people could be a boss, family members, friends, clients, or co-workers. The interesting thing is that if this happens in one area of one's life, the feel-good factor is carried over into other areas. Within reason, the higher our level of self-esteem the more functional we are.

We all need a certain level of self-esteem in order to function without mental illness. A robust sense of self protects us from anxiety and depression and a number of other annoying psychiatric disorders (although too elevated a sense of self-esteem can be a sign of other pathologies). We tend to gravitate to those people, those firms, and those occupations that we believe will give us the most "bang for the buck" in self-esteem terms. And we will work hard to get it.

Increased self-esteem is undoubtedly a powerful motivator. So, what can you, as a law leader, do to use the drive to increase self-esteem among your partners and others in your firm? How can you frame rewards that add to commitment to new behaviors?

Firstly, you can increase the brand recognition of the firm. The greater the brand recognition, the more committed people will feel. Research has shown that people feel better, and are more productive, if they work for an organization that has a significant brand image. If your employees or partners believe that the new behaviors that you are advocating will lead to greater brand recognition, then that will trigger the reward mechanism of the brain and increase self-esteem. Secondly, you can demonstrate that the behavioral changes you advocate will lead to more accolades from clients, colleagues, the public, or even family members. All of these will use the drive for self-esteem to solidify the changes in behaviors and thus mindset that are necessary for the firm to prosper in the new reality.

TOP TIP

**Think carefully about how you will reward behavioral change at the same time you decide on specific changes, and craft the two together.**

## Conclusion

We have discussed at length in this chapter the need to introduce and solidify behavioral changes. Of course, mere behavioral modifications are not enough to change the culture of a firm. But they are an essential start. Culture change, as we pointed out in the previous chapter, requires a change in mindset on the part of partners and employees.

The important take-away from this chapter is that mindset change is only possible as a result of the successful application of new behaviors. Mindset, in other words, is behaviorally based. The most dangerous thing a law leader can do is to assume that their partners and other employees will accept the need for change just because the law leader does. They won't. They will likely resist almost any changes that might impinge upon their nexus of supportive relationships.

The only way to successfully engineer change is to craft a series of rewards that will encourage people to attempt change and then put in place conditions that will inspire people to stick to those changes. The rewards and incentives must be in line with human neurogenetics, they must work with the grain of human nature and not, as with so many so-called incentives, against it.

*A version of this chapter was first published in Murray, B., and Fortinberry, A.,* Leading the Future: The Human Science of Law Firm Strategy and Leadership, *London, ARK Group, 2016*

### *References*

1. Morris, P. and Halkitis, P., "The Influence of context on health", *Behavioral Medicine*, 41, 1–3, 2015.
2. Rosenblatt, Z. et al, "A Gender-based Framework of the Experience of Job Insecurity and Its Effects on Work Attitudes" *European Journal of Work and Organizational Psychology*, 8:2, 1999, pp. 197–217.
3. Avolio, B.J. et al, "The heritability of emergent leadership: Age and gender as moderating factors" *The Leadership Quarterly*, 23:2, 2012, pp. 219–232.
4. Fein, E. et al, "Cognitive basis for corruption and attitudes towards corruption in organizations viewed from a structuralist adult developmental meta-perspective", *Behavioral Development Bulletin*, 19:3, 2014, 78–94.
5. Ertac, S. et al, "Deciding to decide: Gender, leadership and risk-taking in groups" *Journal of Economic Behavior & Organization*, 83:1, 2012, pp. 24–30.
6. Stepien, R. et al, "Biologically inspired models of decision making" in *Advances in Cognitive Neurodynamics*, Springer Science, Drodrecht, 2015, pp. 55–56.
7. Goleman, D. and Boyatzis, R., "Social Intelligence and the Biology of Leadership", *Harvard Business Review*, September 2008.
8. Farmer, N., *The Invisible Organization*, Gower Publishing, Aldershot, 2008.
9. Krawczyk, J. and Steinberg, J., "How Content Is Really Shared: Close Friends, Not 'Influencers'", *Advertising Age*, 7 March 2012.
10. Serrat, O., A *Primer on Social Neuroscience Asian Development Bank*, Washington, DC, 2010.
11. Baumeister, R., "The need to belong: Desire for interpersonal attachments as a fundamental human motivation", *Psychological Bulletin*, 117:3, 1995, 497–429.
12. Baumeister, R. et al "Thwarting the Need to Belong: Understanding the Interpersonal and Inner Effects of Social Exclusion" *Social and Personality Psychology Compass*, 1:1, 2007, 506–520.
13. Anderson, C. et al, "The Local-Ladder Effect: Social Status and Subjective Well-Being" *Psychological Science* 23:7, 2012, pp. 764–771.
14. Bevort, F. and Suddaby, R., "Scripting professional identities: how individuals make sense of contradictory institutional logics", *Journal of Professions and Organization*, 2015.

15. Neiss, M. et al, "Genetic influences on level and stability of self-esteem" *Self and Identity* 5:3, 2006, pp. 247–266.
16. Chavez, R.S. and Heatherton, T.F., "Multimodal frontostriatal connectivity underlies individual differences in self-esteem", *Social Cognitive and Affective Neuroscience*, 10:3, 2015, pp. 364–370.

# Chapter 9:
# Strategic approaches to introducing change

*By Patrick J. McKenna, author, lecturer, strategist, and advisor to the leaders of premier law firms*

The following represents comments that I offered in a recent interview and are based on my three decades of working with large law firms internationally who invariably are trying to execute a particular strategy, implement a new initiative or roll out some new program and feeling frustrated by inevitable, internal resistance.

Change goes against the grain of any firm's status quo. And most law firms have powerful immune systems that throw up multiple barriers to turning new ideas into commercial realities. It takes understanding some of these basic change hurdles and intense perseverance in order to make anything really happen.

### Why do you think firms find change to be so difficult?

I have a very profound answer to that question... Because change is SO bloody difficult!

Now I appreciate that that sounds flippant, but I see many, many firms underestimating just how difficult it really is to bring about change. In particular I see new firm leaders thinking that they can easily change their firm's culture, or get their practice groups operating more effectively, or introduce a new level of client transparency – and then operating as though just willing it to happen will be sufficient.

We have books out there that prescribe eight simple rules you need follow to bring about change. Now that sounds easy, doesn't it? Only problem, according to the most recent research from McKinsey, is that in the twenty years since Professor Kotter's book has been out, the success rate for bringing about change has not improved one little bit – 70 percent of all change initiatives *still fail* (and by the way that's in a corporate "do as I say or you're fired" type environment).

Meanwhile, in professional service firms we continue to see all of these articles that tell law firms, "change or die" like these authors all think that that is supposed to be some kind of motivator. Let's see if I can offer one simple example of the enormity of this change challenge.

Imagine with me for a moment as you are reading this, that heaven forbid, you develop pains in your chest and you have a heart attack... but we quickly get you to a world-class cardiac specialist and you undergo a coronary bypass. Not quite as scary as it once was, as I'm told that over 1.5 million Americans have this surgery every year.

Following your surgery, your doctor tells you that in order for you to prevent pain, avoid a repeat of the surgery, and essentially to prolong your life, you have to adopt a healthier lifestyle: which essentially means no smoking, drinking, over-eating, or stress and you *must* start exercising.

Follow me?

I've related this same scenario to some large audiences that I've had the honor of speaking to, and asked for a show of hands: "How many of you could faithfully follow your doctor's directions?"

Keep in mind, this really is a matter of change or die! And at least 95 percent (if not all) of the hands go up.

But... unfortunately according to Ed Miller, retired CEO at John Hopkins, fewer than 3 percent of those 1.5 million Americans can sustain the change and therefore live beyond a few more years. In most cases less than five years.

And notice that is not a 70 percent failure rate for change. That is a 97 percent failure rate!

Now, I have surveyed firms on this question: think back to some important initiative that didn't quite turn out to be the roaring success that firm leadership had hoped. "What were the primary obstacles your firm faced as it tried to implement the new strategic initiative?" And to help, everyone was given 17 different choices.

The most popular response coming from 94 percent of the respondents and over 74 law firms was that: "They involved changes that some lawyers were not motivated to make." For example: they required a generous amount of non-billable time, or they took lawyers out of their comfort zone, or they threatened to change the status quo of some lawyers in the firm.

Charles Darwin had this famous saying that I think needs to be posted on the wall of every law firm boardroom – "It is not the strongest of the species that survives, nor the most intelligent; it is the one that is most adaptable to change."

**What are some of the more common hurdles you have observed or experienced in bringing about change?**

I look at this question from two levels – the leadership and then the partnership.

### At the top of the firm

An old friend Dr. Jack Zenger has some interesting research accumulated on more than 65,000 leaders/managers measuring 49 various leadership behaviors, with data comparing older, more experienced leaders with their younger counterparts. The bottom line from Jack's research is that leaders, on average, do not become more effective with age. They become more experienced, but not more effective!

Jack's data shows that many older leaders become less receptive to feedback and change over time – while younger leaders seem more inclined to embrace change and exhibit great skills at marketing their new ideas. Now, it probably could be argued that this happens specifically because of the younger leaders' lack the experience (they don't know what they don't know), and that causes them to be more optimistic about their proposals for change. But, nevertheless, it is what it is.

Generally I see older leaders (myself included) who are quick to point to others who resist change. It's much harder to recognize or admit to our own change resistance. And so for anyone who built a firm's past successes, the often (I think unconscious) temptation to preserve the status quo can be overwhelming.

Now, for those senior leaders who really do believe they can bring about change, I see too many change efforts fail simply because firm leadership launches some initiative, then moves straight on to the next topic. That leaves partners wondering if this was really something important or just the flavor of the month. It isn't enough to focus some time on it. Leadership needs to say, "this is our priority and we are going to make darn sure we work long and hard to make things happen".

### Among the partners

One of the things I hear far too often, is this *fear of failure*, of making a mistake. A partner related to me recently about how he was reluctant to pursue exploring a new niche area in self-driving vehicles, because if things should not pan out, he will forever be stigmatized. And that was the precise word he used – *stigmatized*!

I relate this fear of making a mistake to our professional mindset and desire to get things perfect – to get things just right, the very first time

– which is highly desirable in work on behalf of clients, but absolutely paralyzing with anything new or entrepreneurial. In yet, I continually see lawyers striving for perfection from the outset and unwilling to go public until they are entirely happy with the new initiative.

*Competence* is another enemy of change. Many professionals get locked into a successful mode of behavior and naturally resist change because change threatens to make them less competent. As professionals, we all like being competent – that is who we are and sometimes that is all we've got. So just think of the risks that come with embracing anything new. A fresh approach to serving clients, one that would prevent me from maximizing my billable hours and force me to be more productive and practice differently. Yeah... let me think about it.

Finally, all of this manifests itself in too much *short-term thinking* and the pursuit of immediate gratification. Respectfully, I think many firms have atrophied in their ability to think and act strategically. It's all about immediate results. Too many firms seem to have lost the habit of investing in their future.

## What definitely does not work in introducing change?

In my survey of firms, the second question we asked was: Think back to some important initiative that didn't quite turn out to be the roaring success that firm leadership had hoped. "What specific actions did your firm take to try to further this strategic initiative?" Everybody was given another 16 different choices.

For this question, the most popular response from 76 percent was: "Most of what had been done boiled down to multiple emails, memos, presentations and talking points about the need for change."

I think what this clearly indicates is that we continue to subscribe to models for leading change that simply don't work. In this example we find ourselves, (unconsciously perhaps) trying to overwhelm our colleagues with data. We give them facts, statistics, figures, flowcharts in amongst our rousing discourses for why we must, as a successful firm, adapt to some new change.

We like to think that these facts (as we perceive them) will convince partners to change – that our colleagues are essentially rational if given accurate information. How often do you hear someone advise that you need to make a sound "business case" for what needs to be done? So, we believe that if we provide relevant data about the issue, present a business case and sensible recommendations, our colleagues will just immediately take action.

Now if your partners should have doubts or disagree (and you can be assured that many will), we take that as a clear sign that we haven't yet done a good job of presenting the evidence.

So, when partners don't immediately get on-board with any suggested course of action, what do we do?

We try harder to persuade them. We try to give them even more data. We keep doing the same thing... only more of it. And, we *turn up* the volume. We explain it over and over again. After all, you've all heard from those communications experts who tell us that you can never over-communicate your message!

Unfortunately, this seldom seems to work. Because, if we think about it, it's built upon an assumption that I'm right and those of my partners who "simply don't get it" (and how often have you heard or perhaps uttered those words?) or "don't see the light" are wrong. That's an approach that all too often turns the exchange into a contest over whose idea or beliefs will win.

And sometimes even worse, it hardens the views of those opposed: "Hell will freeze over before I get on board with that proposition."

## How do you develop a sense of urgency that gets partners' attention?

Two things I've learned that I think many firms overlook: One is to remember that your partners often come into any new change carrying the baggage of many past failures; and secondly that those partners are often highly skeptical of any change proposals coming from management.

There's this natural skepticism among partners – "here comes another management change initiative." I can report that I've personally witnessed a number of instances where some young, junior professional goes to a senior and asks "what's this all about?" only to hear the senior say "head down, billables up... this too will pass".

When I first started working with law firms some thirty years ago, a very wise, elder statesman, the founder of a rather large firm said to me, "McKenna, there is only one thing that you need to keep in mind if you are going to be successful in consulting to lawyers." I said, "Oh and what is that?" He said, you need to burn this into your brain: "No lawyer ever salutes, endorses, gets excited about, or enthusiastically supports any idea, program, initiative, plan, new direction or change... that they themselves have not been part in formulating".

Therefore the challenge is – how do I get these professionals, my team mates, meaningfully involved in the change that needs to happen, such that they can see their fingerprint somewhere on the final course of action that we are all about to take together.

In other words, people support what which they help create. Too often management is guilty of making a decision then feigning buy-in. That just doesn't work.

Fundamentally, what I see effective firm leaders do, and I've watched this closely over many years, is to essentially frame the problem, issue, situation, or opportunity such that the key question from the firm leadership becomes: "please help us think this through, how do we make this work?" If you close off resistance, you're saying "we've already made our decision, we're not interested in hearing from you".

In other words, the best leaders find ways to get the change out there, subtly, then listen their partners' views and promote as much discussion as possible. They view resistance as a gift rather than a problem. You want to invite resistance, bring it to the surface, make it safe to express. After all, you may not have completely thought through all of the elements of some change initiative. Any resistance may actually offer some suggestions about how to make the change flow even more smoothly.

Some of that may involve one-on-one communication. Keep in mind, that at the most personal level, change equals loss. Every change usually represents a loss of some kind. The loss – real or perceived – might involve esteem, money, status, relationships, or other factors. Who feels threatened that they might be losing something? What is that, and is that threat genuine, or is it just a misperception on their part? And, if it is real, it should be put on the table. Acknowledge there's going to be a loss. Keep nothing hidden.

You only get them on board to the extent that they see that going in the new direction is better than the status quo. You can try to persuade them and we've talked about how well that works. Or you subtly find ways to get them to come to that recognition of their own volition.

One of the most important things I've learned is that any change effort is a numbers game. You're never going to get everyone on board. Abandon that thought right now. To the extent that you get enough of the significant or power partners on board, the rest will follow.

### Can you share some approaches that firm leaders have found to be effective?

As I've seriously studied this for some time, I've identified over 26 different, what I'll call *change levers*, that any leader has at their disposal and that can be utilized to stimulate some "healthy" tension within the firm. No one lever, by itself, is likely to do the job, but utilizing a number of these can make a huge difference.

Let me give you a few real-world examples.

**1. Bring in outside resources to speak on new developments**

I remember one managing partner who very early into his tenure organized a monthly lunch for partners – but attendance was optional. Participants could take part through audio or video conferencing. He would always invite a speaker, for example the managing partner of an accounting firm, an academic doing some relevant research, or an important client. And, speakers were deliberately chosen for their provocative content. It was clear, if you followed where he was going, that he was trying to educate his partners about the changing environment, what was going on out there and subtly direct their attention to very specific issues. Following one of these luncheons the hallways were usually buzzing for days about the particular speaker and the content discussed. That was this firm leader's way of "ripening" particular issues, until pretty soon partners were coming to him and asking him when the firm was going to take action on certain matters. But for him to have led the charge, he would likely have been doomed. So, I think your change initiative often has to be subtle, almost like a political grass roots movement, nurturing, and educating people and getting them to push the call for action.

**2. Launch a pilot project**

Rather than trying to launch a full-blown change effort, start with something small and admit you don't know if it is going to work or not. I've seen this work in a number of firms trying to introduce business development training. They'll say, "We would like you to come and help us assess if this is going to work. We will run a couple of sample sessions, and we need you to sit in wearing two hats; one as a participant and one as someone who will critique this for us." When you give people that kind of power and respect, they take it seriously. You are then in a position to say, "that session didn't work, but did you like the idea? How can we do it differently so it will work?" Now you're not talking about whether we will make the change, do the training, but you have now gravitated to how we will do the training. That's a huge step.

**3. Start a new ritual, ceremony or procedure to shape intended behavior**

They tell a story about the old Reed Smith firm where they were trying to incite partner collaboration. "Being collaborative", by their definition, was that if someone needed help with something, the help was freely given, genuine, and not just because the individual got to bill their time to some client. When you walked into their Pittsburgh reception area they have this huge lion, known as the Shaw Lion. Firm leadership decided to create miniature Shaw Lions, about the size of your fist, made out of pewter. Once a year all the equity partners would vote on that lawyer in the firm who made the greatest contribution to helping them personally and their practice, and they awarded that lawyer the Shaw's Lion. I can report, from having one of those people in a room and discussing the highlight of their professional practice, that I witnessed a lawyer in his early fifties relate to his colleagues about the year he received this award... with tears in his eyes. Talk about emotion driving change and the idea of what you reward! Unfortunately, too many people take that to mean "if we throw money at the issue people's behaviors will change." If you celebrate people's contributions in a public way, that changes behavior.

**4. Show or stimulate examples of what the future might look like**

At a Texas-based firm engaged in some serious strategic planning, the Strategic Planning Committee put out a call out for volunteers – associates and junior partners, roughly between the ages of 30 to 45, to sit on a couple of self-organizing task forces. Each task force was then asked to develop a written scenario to specifically identify in detail, "what the legal profession would look like in the year 2020." They were then asked to present their scenarios at a special partner's meeting which was focused on the theme of "where the firm was going." Words cannot describe how impressed the partners were or how that initiative helped inject new thinking and ideas into the firm's strategic plan.

**5. Initiate an internal survey (identify some troubling concerns/ aspirations)**

One AmLaw 100 firm was particularly troubled when it found itself at the bottom of a published ranking concerning associate dissatisfaction. Recognizing that the results spoke to a need to modify certain aspects of the culture of their organization, the firm turned to Dr. Daniel Dennison one of the leading authorities on organizational culture. With Dennison's help the firm administered a behavioral survey throughout the firm, involving partners, associates, and support staff – identifying the firm's strengths and weaknesses across 60 distinct areas from the importance of core values and the firm's team orientation, to the efforts made to promote professional development and the degree to which innovation was encouraged. The survey allowed the firm to identify specific areas needing remedial attention and created the internal enthusiasm for making small changes that resulted in the firm's associate satisfaction scoring in the top quartile – one year later.

Always keep this in mind. We're likely to take a different approach when we start to think about change from the perspective of: "what would work on me; somebody harping at me, or somebody who leads me to start behaving and/or thinking about an issue in a way that is in my own best interests?"

### How does one fit their leadership style to the challenge?

If I had to choose one thing, and at first blush it may seem simplistic, it would have to be shaping your firm's culture to embrace change. And one way to think about this is in the language that we use – in other words how do we use language to shape our collective thinking. What you do and say as a Leader has far more influence over the success or failure of a change than anything else. Let me tell you what happened to me.

In an earlier life, I was a vice-president and director of a Canadian-based, public company in the telecommunications industry. I had the good fortune of working with a rather progressive, very successful CEO who held some very strong beliefs. One of those beliefs, that he preached to all of his senior team, repeatedly, was that upon first being presented with any new idea or proposed course of action, he would say, "You have 'no intellectual integrity" voicing a personal opinion that suggests that you know whether it will work or not – because the reality is that you do NOT know for certain – and even if that same idea has been tried before – say, only last year – in this firm or some other firm and failed. That still is not determinative of whether the idea will fail here and now".

He taught us that you only display intellectual integrity (he loved that term) by asking and answering three sequential questions:

1. Not, "Will this work", but, "How do we make this work?" (which you will notice provokes a whole different mindset). He believed you start with a focus on "possibility" not "probability" or "profitability";
2. "What's the worst that could happen?" (let's be realistic, where might the crap hit the fan?); and finally,
3. "Where is our back door if the worst that could happen *does* happen?"

Unfortunately, winning the debate, arguing well, finding the slightest little flaw in the ideas of others is often the behavior that seems to be held in great esteem within our firms. And allowing that behavior rarely builds trust or inspires innovation. So to shape a culture that embraces change, I believe starts with the firm leader making it socially unacceptable to *ever* offer an immediate opinion on whether any new idea will work.

In fact, in a number of the practice groups that I have worked with, they have, with my encouragement, adopted a group protocol (a behavioral guideline for self-governing their collective behavior) that states: "we all agree that in our group, we will LOVE every new idea… for five minutes!"

Finally, I think that one of the toughest jobs that the firm leadership has is to maintain momentum, enthusiasm, and demonstrate tenacity. Here are a few very specific actions that I've discovered work within firms:

1. Don't launch and leave – stay laser-focused on executing a few initiatives at a time.
2. Ensure that the change is a regular agenda item on management meetings.
3. Conduct regular meetings of practice leaders – raise issues, cross-fertilize, explore successes, collaborate.
4. Look for some "symbolic" way or act to demonstrate seriousness.
5. Set up a project management center with someone who is knowledgeable about and focused on the human side of the change to:

   (a) Match those struggling with those who have successfully mastered the implementation;

   (b) Respond to criticism, make adjustments, remove obstacles, and push forward.
6. Establish an intranet site for ideas, tools, templates, training modules, and other shared assets.
7. Provide generous amount of coaching, guidance, and support.
8. Market internally any and every visible sign of improvement.
9. Embed the new change into all existing: firm systems, procedures, protocols, training, relationships, etc.
10. Use a single metric that best expresses progress for the entire endeavor with relentless campaign communicating progress.
11. Remind everyone how much has already been accomplished.
12. Conduct post-mortem: working well, not working, needs adjustment (e.g.: a self-administered questionnaire).

www.ingramcontent.com/pod-product-compliance
Ingram Content Group UK Ltd.
Pitfield, Milton Keynes, MK11 3LW, UK
UKHW021848150926
8657IPUK00005B/149

9 781783 583003